The Life of St. Philip Howard

St. Philip Howard
1557 – 1595

The Life of
St. PHILIP HOWARD

First edited by Henry Granville, 14th Duke of Norfolk, E.M. in 1857 from a manuscript at Arundel Castle and now revised, with additional notes

With a Foreword

by

Bernard, 16th Duke of Norfolk, E.M.

Phillimore
London and Chichester

1971
Published by
PHILLIMORE & CO. LTD.
Shopwyke Hall, Chichester, Sussex, England
This edition © 1971
SBN 900592 16 8

188316

9L

A2 84s

Nihil obstat: ✠ David Cashman Bishop of Arundel and Brighton
Censor Librorum: L.E. Whatmore (CENSOR DEPUTATUS)
Imprimatur: ✠ David Cashman Bishop of Arundel and Brighton
Arundel, 3rd December, 1970.

Text set throughout in 12 on 14 point Caslon and printed on 24 basis Antique Laid.
Made and printed in England by Gordon Norwood
at The Roundwood Press Limited
Kineton, Warwick

Contents

Foreword		ix
Abbreviated pedigree showing the descent of St. Philip Howard		x
Introduction		xii
Preface to the First Edition		xv

Chapter		Page
I	His birth and parentage	1
II	His childhood and education	3
III	His going to Court, and the hurt he received by it	5
IV	The occasions of his conversion to the Catholic faith	8
V	The beginning of his troubles	10
VI	His reconciliation to the Church, and change of life	12
VII	His resolution to leave the kingdom, and his letter to the Queen	14
VIII	His taking at sea, and commitment to the Tower	24
IX	His examination and censure in the Star Chamber	26
X	The strictness of his imprisonment, and hard usage therein	30
XI	Other injuries and calumnies during his imprisonment	32
XII	The means and manner how he was entrapped	36
XIII	His examination about that business	38
XIV	His arraignment and condemnation	41
XV	What he did after his condemnation	44
XVI	The manner of his life in the Tower	48
XVII	The occasion of his last sickness, and manner of his death	51

XVIII	His burial, and other accidents after his death	56
XIX	A description of his person, and natural gifts	58
XX	Some of his moral virtues	60
XXI	The care of his conscience, and sorrow for his sins	64
XXII	His constancy in the Catholic faith	68
XXIII	His cheerfulness in suffering, and confidence in God	70
XXIV	His charity and good desires	72
XXV	The great good estimation others had of him	74

Biographical Notes 77

Appendix 82

Illustrations

    St. Philip Howard   *frontispiece*

I   Inscription carved by St. Philip Howard over the fireplace in the Beauchamp Tower, Tower of London

II   Thomas Howard, 4th Duke of Norfolk

III   Mary, Duchess of Norfolk

IV   Signatures of some Elizabethan statesmen

between pages 28 *and* 29

Note. The frontispiece and plates II and III are from portraits, and plate IV is from a document, all at Arundel Castle. They are reproduced by kind permission of His Grace The Duke of Norfolk, E.M., K.G. Plate I is from a photograph supplied by the National Monuments Record.

Foreword

I am much indebted to Mr Francis Steer for the work he has done to bring the manuscript more up to date.

Philip Howard placed his life in the hands of God when he was twenty-seven and died in the Tower ten and a half years later. He became the Venerable in 1886 and was beatified in 1929 and now my greatest ancestor is canonized and joins the Saints in Heaven.

Arundel Park.   Norfolk. E.M.

ABBREVIATED PEDIGREE SHOWING

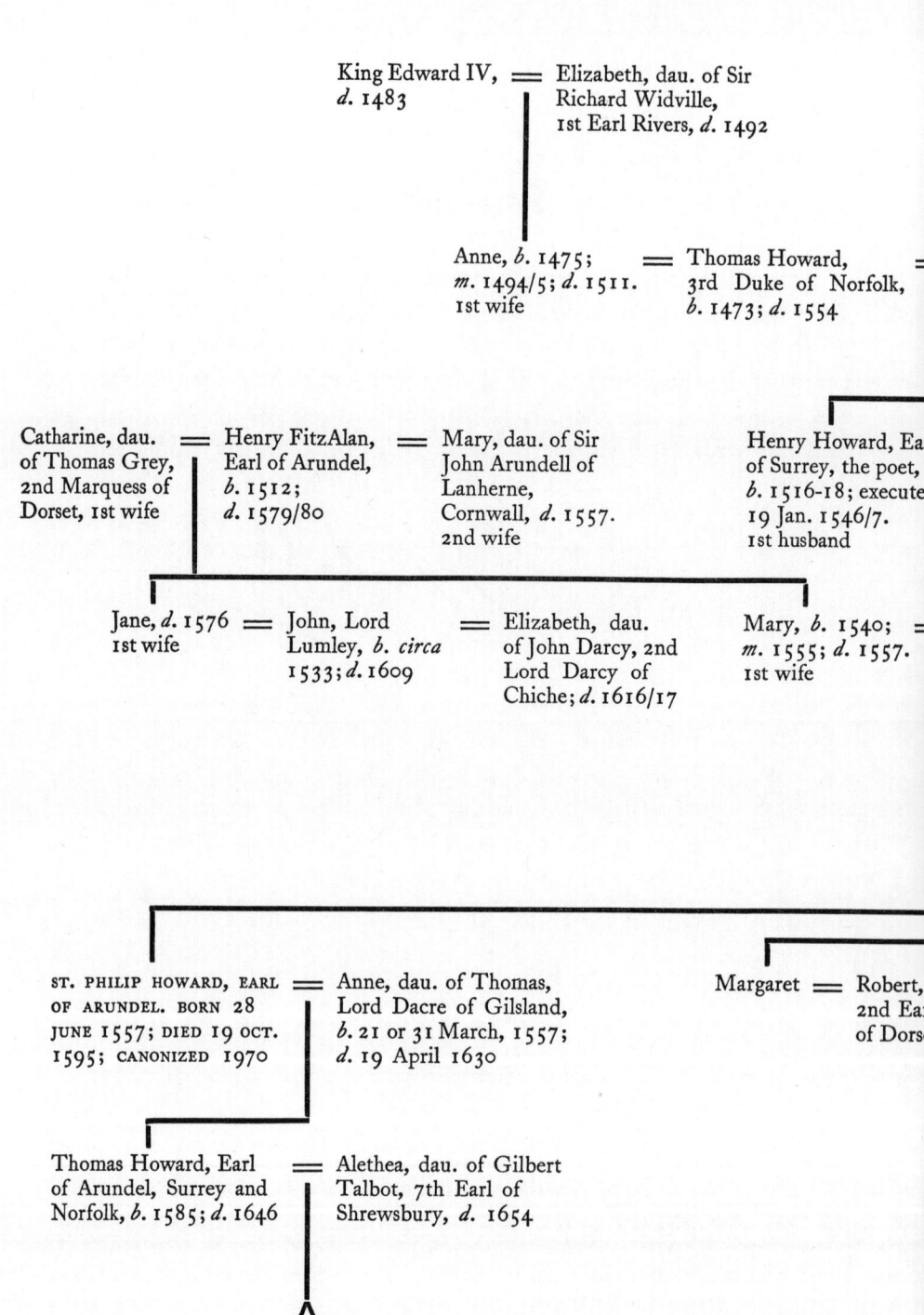

THE DESCENT OF ST. PHILIP HOWARD

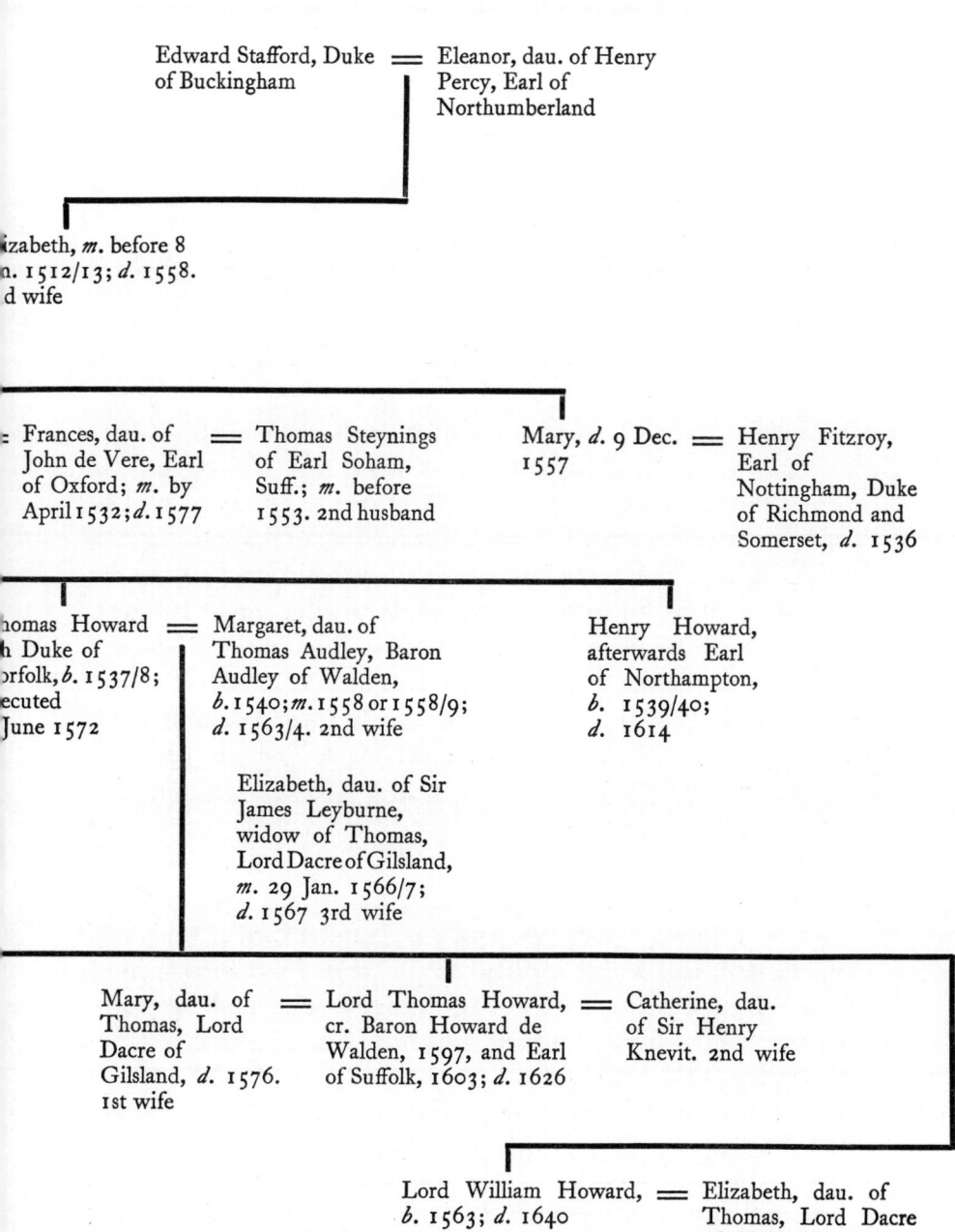

Introduction

THIS edition of the manuscript life of St. Philip Howard, Earl of Arundel is published to mark the canonization of him and thirty-nine other English and Welsh martyrs on 25th October 1970. The manuscript is among the Arundel Castle archives and comprises biographies of the Earl and his wife, Anne Dacre, closely written in an early 18th century hand on 198 pages bound in blue morocco leather to form a book, 19 x 15 cms. The volume is lettered on the spine, *Lives of Phillippe Howard Earl of Arundel and Lady Anne Countesse of Arundel*; at the foot of the spine are the letters M.S. On the inside front cover is a printed label stating the book forms part of the library bequeathed by the will of Edward, Duke of Norfolk, to remain in his family. Edward, 9th Duke of Norfolk, was born in 1686 and succeeded Thomas, his elder brother, in 1732; in 1727 he married Mary, second daughter and coheir of Edward Blount of Blagdon in Devon. The 9th Duke was the builder of the great house at Worksop, Notts., containing 500 rooms which was destroyed by fire in 1761. A great collector of books and manuscripts, the 9th Duke died in 1777 and was buried at Arundel.

It would appear, therefore, that the Arundel Castle version of the biographies is a very careful copy[1] of those first written in or shortly after 1630, the year of the Countess of Arundel's death. The name of the author is unknown, but he was a Jesuit priest and a close friend of the Earl and Countess; he lived with the Countess for almost 14 years during her widowhood. She died at Shifnal Manor, Shropshire and was buried at Arundel.

---

[1] Margaret Waugh, in her monograph, *Blessed Philip Howard, Earl of Arundel and Surrey, Courtier and Martyr* (1961) mentions on p. 9 that a manuscript of the Lives is in the Southwark archives. An enquiry addressed to the Archivist to the Archbishop of Southwark in August 1970, revealed that no such manuscript could be found. Further information as to the whereabouts of this or any other manuscript copies of the Lives would be very welcome.

The biographies of the Earl and Countess were first edited by Henry Granville, 14th Duke of Norfolk and published by Hurst and Blackett of London in 1857; a second edition was issued in 1861. In presenting this new edition, the opportunity has been taken of correcting some minor errors, employing a clearer typeface, and including those innocuous passages which the 14th Duke omitted from his transcript. Brief biographical notes on the persons mentioned in the narrative have been added together with a short pedigree and some illustrations. The life of Anne, Countess of Arundel has not been included in this present edition.

The reason why a completely new life of St. Philip Howard has not been produced is because it seemed appropriate, in this year of the martyr's canonization, to re-issue the biography written by a man who knew him personally. There will be ample opportunity later on for the publication of a full-scale study of his life, influence and times. The Arundel manuscript has been reproduced as precisely as possible although there are many instances where it is doubtful whether a capital or a small letter was intended by the scribe, but no serious damage will result if a wrong decision has been made. Mis-spellings and punctuation have been copied accurately.

The most detailed study of St. Philip Howard so far published was that issued by the Catholic Record Society in 1919 under the title, *The Ven. Philip Howard Earl of Arundel, 1557-1595,* consisting of evidences (including copious extracts from the *Lives*) collected and edited by John Hungerford Pollen, S. J. and William MacMahon, S. J. Other biographies of the Earl are by M. A. Tierney in *The History and Antiquities of the Castle and Town of Arundel* (1834), pp. 357-413; G. Ambrose Lee, *The Life of the Venerable Philip Howard, Earl of Arundel and Surrey* (Catholic Truth Society, 1887); C. Kerr, *The Life of the Venerable Philip Howard* (1926); M. Waugh, *Blessed Philip Howard, Earl of Arundel and Surrey, Courtier and Martyr* (1961); and F. J. Bowen, *Philip of Arundel: a drama in four acts* (n.d.). Extensive use has been made of the *Dictionary of National Biography,* the *Complete Peerage,* and J. Gillow, *A Literary and Biographical History, or Bibliographical Dictionary of the English Catholics,* in the preparation of the biographical notes.

This introduction has been kept brief so as to avoid the difficulties which would inevitably have arisen if an attempt had been made to describe anything other than the provenance of the manuscript and the method of editing it.

I would like to thank His Grace The Duke of Norfolk for contributing a Foreword and for giving me the privilege of preparing a new edition of a book which his grandfather had seen fit first to make available to the public 113 years ago.

Chichester,
December, 1970

F.W.S.

Preface to the First Edition

I TRUST the following Lives will be read with interest. They are given from a Manuscript in my possession, which I have copied with the most careful attention both to its spelling and punctuation. I have not made the smallest alteration except in the 12th and 76th pages, where certain passages have been for obvious reasons omitted, and in the 13th page, where a slightly different construction of the text has enabled me to save a portion of that page which I should otherwise have omitted. I should not, however, have made even these slight alterations but for the advice of a friend.

NORFOLK, E. M.

ARUNDEL CASTLE,
Feast of St Philip Neri.
1857.

CHAPTER I

His Birth & Parentage

AMONGST the many Noble Families of this Kingdome, no one has been more famous, or more illustrious in these latter times, than that of the Howards; nor in it any more worthy of memory than the Lord Philippe Howard Earl of Arundel and Surrey, who was born at Arundel house in London upon S. Peter the Apostle's Eve being ye 28 of June in the year of our Lord 1557, and the fourth of the Reign of the Vertuous Queen Mary of worthy memory for her Piety and Religion.

His Father was Thomas the last Duke of Norfolk who by the appointment of Queen Elizabeth was beheaded upon the Tower hill in the year 1572, and the fourteenth of her Reign. He was a Prince of a very moderate Disposition and moral good Life, tho' not a little infected with Heresy by reason of his Education in his Aunt the Duchesse of Richmond's house, which was a receptacle & harbor of pernicious persons tainted in that kind, and in particular of the Infamous Apostat John Bale, as also of John Fox the Author of that pestilent book called *Acts and Monuments*.

His Mother was the Lady Mary Fitzallen younger daughter and heire of Henry Fitzallen the last Earl of Arundel of that name, who died in her childbed of him, being not then full 17 years of age, to the incredible grief of the Earl her Father, the Duke her Husband, & all their friends she being of so sweet & amiable disposition, so prudent, pious, Vertuous & Religious, that all who knew her could not but love and esteem her much, and consequently lament the loss of her.

He was baptis'd a few dayes after his Birth in the Chappel of the Queen's Pallace of Whitehall with great Solemnity, The King, Queen, and all the Principal Persons of the Court being there present. The Ceremony was performed by that Worthy Prelat Doctor Nicolas Heath then Archbishop of York & Chancellor of the Kingdome, in a font of gold made of purpose & kept in the Treasury only for the Christening of the children of the Princes of the Realm. His Godfathers were the King Philippe himself of whom he receiv'd his name, & it was the last publick act the King did before his going to the besieging & taking of Saint Quintin in France, for that very day he departed thitherward and never after returned to this Kingdome. The other was his Grandfather the Earl of Arundel, to whom afterwards for want of Issue male he did succeed in that title & Estate. And the Old Duchesse of Norfolk his great Grandmother was the Godmother.

After the death of his mother the Duke his Father married Mrs Margaret Audley, the sole Daughter and Heir of Sir Thomas Audley of Walden in Essex Knight & Baronite, who had been Ld Chancellor in the time of King Henry the Eight, and by her he had two sons, the Lord Thomas Howard, who after was created Earl of Suffolk by King James. And the Lord William Howard who is yet living. And one Daughter, the Lady Margaret who was married to Mr Robert Sackvil Son and Heir to the then Lord Buckhurst, & after Earl of Dorset, & Treasurer of the Realm.

The Duke after the death of his second wife married the third time the Lady Dacres Daughter of Sir James Labourn a Knight of Lancashire, and widow to the Lord Dacres of ye North. And she having one Son, & three Daughters, the Duke intended to have married his Daughter the Lady Margaret to that Son ; & his three Sons after the Death of that yong Lord Dacres (who was slain casually at Thetford by the fall of a vaulting hors upon him) to her three Daughters. As in effect the Earl of Surrey his Eldest was to Ann her eldest, and the Lord William to Elizabeth ye youngest.

CHAPTER II

His Childhood & Education

I NEED not here express the great Care the Duke his Father had of him during his infancy and Childhood, as being his Eldest Son, and heir both of his own house, and that of his Grandfather the Earl of Arundel. It will be sufficient to signify how he appointed a grave and ancient Gentlewoman to have the overseeing & Looking to him during his Infancy, & some others to teach him the first rudiments of Learning until he came to be of sufficient Capacity for further teaching, the which in him was sooner than ordinary by reason of his natural vivacity and forwardness of wit.

For that purpose and for his better Education, the Duke made choice of Mr Gregory Martin Fellow at that time of St John's College in Oxford a man of great Learning and knowledge especially in the Greek & Hebrew tongues, & of extraordinary modesty & moderation in his behaviour. But he being wholy Catholick in his Judgment and affection, either could not, or would not stay with him after that the Duke in time of his troubles had given order that certain forward Ministers should preach unto his houshold and family, and that all therein should frequent Service, Sermons, and the like: and either then or soon after he resolv'd to become Catholick & go beyond seas, where he was afterwards made Priest, writ divers learned books in defence of Catholick Religion, lived very vertuously and died happily. The Earl during that time he had the Charge of him profited much in his learning, and by that he then saw in him, and hear'd of him, he was afterwards much furthered towards his conversion to the Catholick Faith.

As soon as he came to the age of twelve years complete, he was by the appointment of his Father, & his own free consent publickly marry'd or betrothed to Mrs Ann Dacres eldest Daughter & heir, as was said before, of the Lord Dacres of the North, her mother the Duke's third wife being dead some years before. And about two years after that when he was at years of full Consent, that is, after fourteen complete they were married again by special order from the Duke then Prisoner in the Tower, out of fear lest the first marriage as being made before his Son was come to perfect age, might be annulled by Order of the Queen, or some other means, as not without reason he might suspect some would attempt it should, had it not been made past breaking by iterating ye Contract the second time.

Not long after his Father's death which happen'd in the year 1572, when he was about 15 years of age together with his two younger brothers he went to the University of Cambridge, and remain'd there two years or thereabouts : what benefit he reaped by his being there in matter of learning, I cannot well affirm ; but Certain it is, that in other respects he receiv'd no smal detriment, partly by the bad example he there saw, partly by the liberty permitted him, but principally by ye flattery of some ministers, the which was so palpable sometimes that his Lady has often told me she was ashamed to hear it.

CHAPTER III

His going to Court, & the hurt he receiv'd by it

About the eighteenth year of his age he went to Court, where he was drawn into many great inconveniences: as first into some wanton conversations by the allurements of corrupted immodest young women wherewith the Court in those times did too much abound; for which after his Conversion he shew'd much sorrow, and in part of satisfaction, as himself signify'd in a Letter out of the Tower to Father Robert Southwell of the Society of Jesus, who then liv'd with his Lady, and afterwards was a glorious Martir, intended at his going out to have distributed to the poor all the money which could have been made of such rings, Jewels, and other tokens, which had been given, sent, or presented to him by any persons of that condition. And so free was he ever after from that youthfull vice, that he could, and upon a Just occasion did protest in another Letter to ye same Father, that after he became a member of the holy Catholick Church he never had carnal knowledge of any woman but his wife.

Secondly. Not long after his being at Court, he began first to neglect his wife, seldome either comeing or sending to visit her: and after some time in a manner to reject her, by signifying and saying unto some, that he knew not whether she were his wife or no, and so wholy absenting himself from her, as if really he had not so reputed her. The occasion of this was, a great desire he had to give contentment to the Queen: for having understood by some who had caus'd his Nativity to be calculated, that he shou'd be in great danger to be overthrown by a woman (the which he interpreted to be no other than the Queen) he endeavour'd by all means to get and keep her favour: and because he well perceived she could not endure his Lady (nor indeed the wife of any one to whom she shew'd any special grace) thereupon he neglected her in such manner as was notorious to all who knew them, & seem'd to cast those doubts whether she were his wife or no, tho' for more sureness they had been twice married, as I have said, and as man and wife had liv'd some years in house togather. But those shews of doubt lasted not long: for soon after his Grandfather the Earl of Arundel's death, which happen'd in the year 1580, he came & cohabited with her about the three and twentith year of his age, and had two children by her, a son who is now Earl of Arundel, and a Daughter who died young. And after his becoming Catholick he used her exceeding well, was very repentant for his unkind and hard usage of her, and often ask'd her pardon for it, as shall hereafter be declared.

Thirdly. He was induced by the bad counsel of some he met with at Court, set on secretly, as was thought, by higher power, to neglect his duty in a manner wholy to the Earl his Grandfather, and to behave himself in such manner towards his Aunt the Lady Lumley, as caus'd much grief to her, and much disgust to the Earl her Father, who much loved & esteem'd her as she well deserv'd for her vertue & discretion, and by that means they both were so aversed from him, that they alienated unto others a great part of their Estates which otherwise would have come from them to him. If the Earl his Grandfather's Estate had descended entirely upon him, it join'd to his Father's and to that Part of the Dacres land which he possessed in right of his wife, would have made him of the greatest wealth & power without Comparison of any Subject in the Realm. And therefore the Queen, or some politick persons about her, fearing he might be too great, used such means, that by evil counsel he was drawn into courses so displeasing to his Grandfather & Aunt, that they left him but little in comparison of that which otherwise they would.

Lastly. By his following of the Court he wasted a great part of that Estate which was left him, by profuse expences of great Summs of money in diverse Tiltings & Tourneys made upon the anniversary dayes of the Queen's Coronation to please her, and at the entertainment of Certain great Embassadors, as also by the entertaining of the Queen her self, first at his house of Keninghall in Norfolk, where for divers dayes he lodged & feasted not only her self, & all her family, the Council, Courtiers, and all their Company, but all the Gentlemen also, & people of the Country, who came thither upon that occasion, in such plentifull, bountifull, & splendid manner, as the like had never been seen before in those Countrys. And after, he did the like at his house in Norwich the same Summer when she came thither in progress to see that City & Country. So deeply by these means he came to be indebted, that in many years after he was scarce able to clear himself of them, & in fine could not do it without Sale of a good quantity of both his own, & his Lady's Lands.

CHAPTER IV

The Occasions of his Conversion to the Catholick Faith

THE Inconveniences mentioned in the precedent chapter were very great, into all which he fell by following the Court: But there was another far greater than them all, which proceeded from the same, to wit; a total neglect of his duty to Almighty God. For during all that time, he was so carry'd away with Company, youthfull entertainments, pleasures and delights, that his mind being wholy possess'd with them, & other worldly vanities, he did scarce so much as think of God (as himself afterwards acknowledged) or of any thing concerning Religion, or the Salvation of his Soul: until by the Providence of God it so happen'd that he was present at the disputation which was made in the Tower of London in the year 1581 concerning diverse points of Religion betwixt F^r Edmond Campion of the Society Mr Sherwin & some other Priests of the one part; Charke, Fulk, Whitakers & some other protestant Ministers of the other. For by that he saw & heard there, he easily perceiv'd on which side the truth, & true Religion was, tho' at that time, nor untill a year or two after, he neither did nor intended to embrace & follow it: and after he did intend it a good while passed before he did execute it. For, as himself signify'd in a letter which he afterwards writ in the time of his Imprisonment in the Tower to F^r Southwell, he resolved to become Catholick long before he could resolve to live as a Catholick, and thereupon he defer'd the former untill he had an intent & resolute purpose to perform the latter. The which (being aided by a special grace of God) he made walking one day alone in the gallery of his Castle at Arundel: where after a long and great conflict within himself, lifting up his eies and hands to heaven, he firmly resolved to become a member of Gods Church, and to frame his life accordingly; yet kept it secret, neither making his Lady, nor any other person living acquainted therewith. Untill after some few dayes going to London & meeting his brother the Lord William Howard to whome he bore a special love, he discover'd his determination to him tho' somewhat covertly, & after he had lent him a Catholick book to read wch was written not long before by Mr Doctor Allen, he dealt so efficaciously with him, that he also resolved to be a Catholick.

CHAPTER V

The Beginning of his troubles

THEY having both of them made this determination of becomeing Catholicks, because the times were then exceeding troublesome, and they did apprehend great danger in declareing themselves for such within the Kingdome, therefore after much consultation they resolv'd secretly to leave the land, & with only one gentleman in their company (Mr Nicolas Walgrave) to pass into flanders & there to remain till more quiet times.

His Secretary Mr John Momford who was already then a Catholick and acquainted with their resolution, the Earl did send to Hull in Yorkshire with order to embark himself from thence into some part in Flanders & there to meet him, or expect his comeing: But he before he could get passage there, being apprehended and carry'd before the Earl of Huntington then President of York, could not perform his Lord's command; but was compell'd to return to London back again, where he found him not yet gon, but makeing preparation to receive the Quen at Arundel house upon notice given him that she intended ere long to come thither for her recreation.

A very great & sumptuous banquet he made her when she came, wherewith at that time she seem'd very well contented & gave him many thanks for her entertainment there: but not long after she shew'd little gratitude for it, sending a command he should not go any whither out of that house, but remain therein as Prisoner, giveing also commission to the Lord Hunsdon (who in former times had been the Duke his Father's Page & now was his great enimy) to examin him about his religion, whereof the Queen began to have him in suspition, also about Cardinal Allen, & the Queen of Scots Mother to King James. Whereto in all things he answer'd so wise and warily, that the Lord had no mind to molest him any more with any such demands.

But about a month after Sir Christopher Hatton, who at that time was Captain of ye Guard sent for Mr John Momford and asked him diverse dangerous questions Concerning the Earl, ye Countesse his wife, & his brother the Ld William, as also of himself whether he were a Priest or no. To which he answerd that he neither knew, nor ever heard any hurt at all of any of those honourable persons, & that himself was neither Priest, nor worthy so great a dignity. That night he was committed to close custody and the next day he was examin'd again upon seventeen interrogatories, in all which he ever clear'd himself, the Earl, his Lady, and Brother from all suspition of such crimes as were surmised of them.

The day following he was examin'd the third time, & whilst he was in examination, upon the suddain unexpectedly, the Queen, the Earl of Leicester and diverse others of the Council came into the house to understand, as it seems, what he had confessed. Sir Christopher told them what answer he had made to every thing, but they not resting satisfy'd therewith caus'd him after many threats of racking and other tortures, to be sent prisoner to the Gatehouse, where he was kept some months so close, that none might speak or come unto him. After which time he was carry'd to Whitehall, & there again most straitly examined by the Earl of Leicester, the Ld Hunsdon, Sr Francis Walsingham then Secretary to the Queen, & some other of the Council. Norton the rack master being present who falsly accused him of many things, & objected great matters against the Earl and his Lady affirming him to be privy to them all. But by his answers he so cleared himself, & declared their innocencey, that within a short time they were all set at liberty, & not long after Norton their accuser for some heinous offences was cast into the Tower of London where he died miserably.

CHAPTER VI

His Reconciliation to the Church, and Change of Life

By occasion of those troubles the Earl had defer'd his reconciliation to the Church of God, which he very earnestly desired: but could not put in execution for want of means & oportunity. So soon therefore as they were a little overpassed, he used such diligence therein, that he procured a meeting with Father William Weston a very vertuous and religious Priest of the Society of Jesus well known in England by the name of F^r Edmonds, & much esteem'd in it & other Cuntries for his constant suffering of 17 years imprisonment in the Tower of London, Wisbich & other places for the Profession of the Catholick Religion.

When he was first taken, & put prisoner in the Clinck, the Countesse of Arundel went in disguise to visit him, and offering by means of money to procure his banishment, as was usual in those times, his answer was, as she her self told me, that he was not committed to prison for money, so neither would he be released by money, but expect till either God, or they by whose authority he was deprived of his liberty should of their own accord set him free as he was afterwards at the Entrance of King James, who sent him with some others into banishment wherein he ended his dayes at the City of Vallodolid in Spain with opinion of great sanctity.

By this good man was the Earl reconciled in the year 1584, & by his means receiv'd such comfort to his soul as he never had felt before in all his life, & such good directions for the amending & ordering of his life, as afterwards did greatly help & farther him therein. For, ever after that time he lived in such manner, as that he seem'd to be chang'd into another man, having great care & vigilance over all his actions, and addicting himself much to piety and devotions. For which purpose forthwith he procured to have a Priest ever with him in's own house, by whome he might frequently receive the Holy Sacraments, & dayly have the Comfort to be present at the Celebration of the Holy Sacrifice, whereto with great humility and reverence he himself in person many times would serve.

CHAPTER VII

His Resolution to leave the Kingdome, and his Letter to the Queen

THIS so great change in his manner of life was soon noted & observed by some Courtiers & potent men, who thereupon began mainly to suspect him to be what he was indeed, and some who were his evillwillers did intend to make that as a means to work his ruin & overthrow. At lest he was so inform'd of them, & giving credit thereunto he began again to think of leaving the Kingdome and going into France, where he thought he might both live more safely, & serve God more quietly. Father Weston did all he could to diswade him from that course, as himself told me more than once, but either his own fear, or some other mens persuasions were more prevailing, he resolved to go, & with as much privacy, as possibly might be, in so much that he did not acquaint his Lady therewith, who by some other means having got notice thereof did very earnestly desire to have gon with him. But because she then was with child of her Son, & for some other reasons, he, not thinking it then convenient, persuaded her to stay behind him, assureing her that afterwards he would take such order that she should follow him.

And because he did think that his Enimies after his departure would by their slanderous reports endeavour to disgrace him with the people & cause the Queen to have sinister surmises of him, he writ a long letter to her which he left with his Sister the Lady Margaret Sackvil to be delivered unto her after his arrival in France, by which it might appear both to her & all others, what were the true causes moving him to undertake that resolution. The tenor thereof was as follows:

May it please your most Excellent Majesty.

As the displeasure of a Prince is a heavier burden to bear, than the hard conceit of a meaner & inferior person : so it is not lawfull for any, & less convenient for them to settle an opinion of mislike before either there appear some cause sufficient to procure it, or there be a fault committed worthy to deserve it. I speak not this, that I doubt of your Majesty's gratious disposition, or that I fear you will condemn me without just & evident proof (for I know it agrees with the honour of your Estate, and I can witness it hath been the manner of your proceedings to know the cause before you give the censure and to hear the matter, before you condemn the person) but I speak with humility, that I may receive this favourable and indifferent dealing at your Majesty's hands : because as I am most desirous to conserve your gratious and good opinion, so am I most earnest to remove all impediments that may hinder or withdraw the fame. And besides, for that many actions at the first shew may seem rash and unadvised, which after ripe & sufficient consideration of the cause, do appear to be just & necessary. I most humbly beseech your most Excellent Majesty to vouchsafe but the reading of this simple writing, and in allowing me this (which is no more than your Majesty's place doth require you to bestow upon your meanest Subjects, & the gratiousness of your nature hath alwayes moved you to grant to every sutor) your Majesty shall do a thing which is pleasing in the sight of God, & honourable in the eies of ye world you shall take a course which is worthy of your self and do that Justice which appertaineth to your estate : to be short, I doubt not by this means both your Majesty shall rest satisfy'd in seeing the true & full defence of my dealing, & I reremain[1] happy, being delivered from all fear and suspition of your displeasure.

And because the course of my former life may in some part express the reason of my present fact, I most humbly beseech y^r Majety y^t with favour I may put in remembrance how since my first comeing to the Court which is nine or 10 years past at the least, it hath been my chiefest care to perform that which I thought might most content you, how I have been alwayes ready and ever

---

[1] *sic.*

willing to do you that service, which either duty required at my hands, or the smalness of my ability would permitt. Your Majesty best knoweth, and for proof thereof I will appeal to no other Judge than your self, tho' I could justly call a great part of your Realm to be witness herein. And so happy I was before some years, in that it pleased your Majesty to accept my service in gratious part, and to conceive a favourable opinion of all mine actions, as I accounted the labours I took a comfort. I made my self a stranger to my own hous to be a continual waiter upon your Ma^{ty}, and liked to live in any sort at the Court, rather than in the best manner at home: for I thought my self happiest when I was nearest to your Ma^{ty}, & my time best spent, when I bestow'd it in doing of your service. But at the last whether the malice of mine adversaries by reason of your Majesty's good Countenance towards me, did begin to be greater than it was, or their credit with your Ma^{ty} for my mishap did grow to be more than in times past it had been, I know not: but I did find by little and little your good opinion declined, and your favours, as I thought, somewhat estranged from me. I heard from time to time how your Ma^{ty} took exceptions at many of my actions, & how it pleased you dayly in your discourses to bewray an hard and evil opinion of me. I saw that such as evermore you hated in your heart and those which before you had not favour'd, did winne your Ma$^{ty's}$ good countenance, which till that time they could by no means obtain, and besides that, received protection and assistance from y^r Ma^{ty} in all their actions against me, presently after they had offer'd me wrong, & were become my adversaries.

Notwithstanding all this I knowing my conscience to be clear came at convenient times to do my duty to your Ma^{ty}, & tho' it pleased you at some times to talk with me, yet your Ma^{ty} never charged me with the least fault or offence unto you; and those adversaries of mine, who did bark behind my back durst never accuse me, nor once open their mouths to my face. So that I accounted my hap very ill, that I was wrongfully accused, but much worse, because at no time I was openly charg'd, whereby I might have had a just occasion both to have shew'd mine Innocency, & to have satisfy'd your majesties suspition. For first; seeing your Ma^{ty} to countenance my adversaries who seek of purpose to disgrace me, & that you would not many times in their presence vouchsafe so much as once bend your eies to the place where I stood. Secondly, I finding them encouraged to mine Injury diverse wayes by ye help of your favour, my self being unable to defend my self any wayes by reason of your displeasure. Lastly, perceiving by your Majesties open disgrace, which all men did note, & by your bitter Speech, which most men did know, that I was generally accounted, nay that I was in a manner pointed at as one whome your Majesty did least favour, & most disgrace, & as a person whome you did deeply suspect, & especially mislike I knew this smoke did bewray a fire, & I saw these clouds did foretell a storm, & therefore I prepared my self with patience to endure whatsoever it was the will of God by means of your Maties indignation to lay upon me, being assured that my faults towards you were none, though mine offences towards others were many. And thus having resolved my self to endure whatsoever should happen : I continued some months in this deep disgrace without either knowing what was the ground of your Maties displeasure, or hearing what should be the end of my own misfortune : till at last I was called at your Majesties Commandment before your Council at two several times, where many things were objected against me, & some of them such trifles, as they were ridiculous, others of them could not be justify'd. And yet notwithstanding that mine Innocency did so evidently appear by mine answers, as my greatest adversaries could not reprove me of the smalest offence or undutifullness to your Majesty, I was commanded to keep my house wherefore I saw it was resolved by the course of this dealing that how clear or manifest soever mine Innocency was my adversaries should receive the triumph of the Victory in having what they would, & I feel the disgrace of mine own misfortune in endureing that, which no way I deserved, & mine enimies to maintain their doing by some colourable shew, seeing they could not Justifie their accusations by any sufficient proof, procured that your Ma^{ty} should send some of your Council four dayes after my restraint to examin me of new matters, which were of greater weight, and importance ; but as improbable as the former and I discharged my self, as clearly as of the other before mentioned, so as mine Innocency did more plainly appear, altho' my restraint did continue. For, after this my last examination, I remained in the same estate fifteen weeks at the least; no man charging me with the least offence, nor my conscience being able to accuse me of the smalest fault. And at the last, when either mine enimies could not for shame longer continue their unconscionable proceedings, or that your Ma^{ty} was informed by some of my friends, that I had too long endured this punishment, I was restored to my former liberty without hearing any just cause of your Majesties hard conceit, or any good colour why I was committed, or but ye shadow of a fault which I might be touched with.

Wherefore after I had escaped safely these storms & when I was clearly delivered from all my troubles, I began to call to remembrance the heavy sentence which had lighted upon those three of mine Ancestors, who immediately went before me. The first being my great grandfather, who was so free from all suspition & shew of any fault, as because they had no colour of matter to bring him to his answer, they attainted him by act of Parliament, without ever calling him to his answer. The second being my Grandfather was brought to his tryal, & condemned for such trifles as amazed the standers by at that time, & it is ridiculous at this time to hear the same, nay he was so faultless in all respects as the Earl of Southampton that then was, being one of his greatest enimies fearing lest his innocency would be a mean to save his life, told Sir Christopher Heydon (being one of his Jury) before hand, that tho' he saw no other matter weighty enough to condemn him ; yet it were sufficient reason to make him say guilty, for that he was an unmeet man to live in a commonwealth. The last being my Father was arraign'd according to the law & condemned by his Peers. God forbid that I should think but that his Tryers did that whereunto their consciences did lead them. And yet give me leave I most humbly beseech your Ma^{ty} to say thus much that howsoever he might unwittingly or unwillingly be drawn into greater danger than himself did either see or imagin : yet all his actions did plainly declare & his greatest enimies must of necessity confess, y^t he never carry'd any disloyal mind to your Ma^{ty} nor intended any undutifull act to his Country. & when I had in this sort both fully & throughly considered the fortune of those three which were past I called to mind mine own danger wch was present, & did think it not impossible by the shew of this rough beginning, but I might as well follow them in their fortune, as I have succeeded them in their place. For I considering the greatness of mine enimies power to overthrow me; & in the weakness of my self, no ability to defend me, I perceived in my late trouble how narrowly my life was fought, & how easily your Ma^ty was drawn into a suspitious & hard opinion of my Ancestors, & by my past dangers how mine Innocency was no sufficient warrant to protect my self. I knew my self, & besides was charged by your Council to be of that Religion, which they accounted odious, & dangerous to your state. Lastly, but principally I weigh'd in what miserable & doubtfull case my soul had remained, if that my life had been taken, as it was not unlikely by former troubles: for I protest the greatest burden that rested in my conscience at that time was because I had not liv'd according to the prescript rule of that which undoubtedly I believe & assuredly presume to be the truth.

Wherefore being somewhat induced by all these reasons, but chiefly moved by this last argument, I thought that the not performing of my duty towards God in such sort as I knew w^d please him best, might be a principal occasion of my late punishment: and therefore resolved whilst I had oportunity to take the course which might be sure to save my soul from the danger of shipwrack altho' my body were subject to ye peril of misfortune. And ever since I followed & pursued this good intent of mine, tho' I perceiv'd somewhat more danger to mine estate, yet I humbly thank God I have found a great deal more quietness in my mind. And in this respect I have just occasion to esteem my past troubles as my greatest felicity. For both of them were (tho' indirectly) the means to lead me to that course, which ever brings perfect quietness, & only procures eternal happyness. And being resolved rather to endure any punishment then willingly to decline from the beginning I had begun, I did bend myself wholy as near as I could to continue in the same without any act which was repugnant to my Faith & Profession. And by means hereof was compelled to do many things which might procure peril to my self, & be an occasion of mislije unto your Majesty: for the first day of this Parliament when your Ma^ty with all your Nobility was hearing of a Sermon in the Cathedral Church of Westminster above in the Chancel, I was driven to walk by my self below in one of the Isles.

And one day this last lent when your Ma^ty was hearing another Sermon in ye Chappel at Greenwich, I was forced to stay all that while in the presence chamber. To be short, when your Ma^ty went upon any Sunday or Holyday to your great closet, I was forced to stay either in the privy chamber, & not to wait upon you at all, or els presently to depart as soon as I had brought you to the Chappel. These things & many more I could by no means escape, but only by an open plain discovery of my self in the eye & opinion of all men as the true cause of my refusal, neither could it long be hidden, altho' for a while it were not generally noted & observed.

Wherefore since I saw that of necessity it must shortly be discover'd, & with all remember'd what a watchfull and jealous eye was carry'd over all those who were known to be recusants, and therewithall calling to mind how all their lodgings were continually searched, & to how great danger they were subject, if a Jesuit or Seminary Priest were found within their houses. I began to consider that either I could not serve God in such sort as I had professed, or else I must incurre the hazard of greater punishment than I was willing to endure. I stood resolute & unremoveable in the first, tho' it were with danger of life, & therefore did apply my mind to devise what means I could for avoiding of the last. Long I was debateing with my self what course to take. For when I consider'd in what continual danger I did remain here in England both by the Laws heretofore establish'd & by a new act lately made, I did think it the safest way to depart out of the Realm, and abide in some other place, where I might live without danger of my Conscience, without offence to your Majesty, without this servil abjection to mine enimies, & without the dayly peril to my life. And yet I was drawn by such forcible persuasions to be of another opinion, as I could nor easily resolve on which part to ground & settle my determination. For on the one side my native Country, my friends, my wife & Kinsfolkes did invite me to stay: on ye other side, the misfortune of my house, the power of my adversaries the remembrance of my former troubles, and the knowledge of my present danger did hasten me to go. And in the end I found no middle course, but either I must venture to live in extreme poverty abroad, or to be sure to remain in continual danger at home. I regarded more the hazard of my life, wherein stood the peril of my

Estate, & I rather sought the preservation of my life, than the profit of my living. Wherefore after I had weigh'd as many dangers as I could remember, and was perswaded that to depart the Realm was the safest way I could take, I did resolve to take the benefit of a happy wind to avoid the violence of a bitter storm, and knowing that the dealing of those who go beyond seas tho' their intent be never so good and dutifull, were yet evil thought of: I presumed to write this Letter to your Ma^{ty}, and in it to declare the true causes and reasons of my departure, both to remove all occasions of doubt & suspition from your Ma^{ty}, which otherwise this suddain departure of mine might Procure. And also to settle as much as lyeth in me your good & gratious opinion of me, which as I have been most desireous to enjoy, so will I be most willing to deserve: and because my adversaries may take this as a fit opportunity to bewray their malice, & kindle your Majesty's indignation against me, I most humbly beseech your Ma^{ty} to ask such as you do think do hate me most, whether being of that Religion which I do professe, & standing every way in the state & condition wherein I did remain, they would not have taken that course for safety of their soules, & discharge of their consciences which I did. And either they must directly tell you that they would have done the same, or acknowledge themselves plainly to be meer Atheists, which howsoever they be affected in their harts, I think they would be loath to confess with their mouths: & when they have satisfied your Ma^{ty} in this point which is the first, I beseech you to ask them of the second, wch is the last. Whether having had their house so fatally & so successively touched, and finding themselves to be of that Religion which is accounted dangerous & odious to the present State, whether having been hardly handled, long restrain'd, & openly disgraced heretofore for nothing, & might now be drawn for their consciences into great & continual danger. Whether having some in chiefest credit with your Majesty their mortal & profess'd enimies, & standing suspected in your Ma$^{ty's}$ opinion both in respect of their father who was taken away in your Ma$^{ty's}$ time, & of themselves who have been since many wayes wronged & injured, & besides being of that Religion which your Ma^{ty} doth detest & of which you are most jealous & doubtfull. To be short, whether haveing had one of their Ancestors taken away without shadow of any fault, but only for this Cause that he was thought to be an unmeet man to live in a com'onwealth at that time, & knowing themselves to be so reputed at this time of those who do bear the most sway in your Ma^{ty's} government. Lastly whether not being able to do any act or duty whereunto their Religion did bind them without the incurring the danger of felony by a new act now lately made, they would have departed out of the Realm, as I have done or no : & either they must say they would joyfully run upon their own death headlong, which is repugnant to the law of God, & contrary to the law of nature as I think, flatly against their own conscience : or els they must acknowledge they would have sought the same means which I have used for the escaping those perils. And then I hope your Ma^{ty} will not hardly conceive of this my dealing, which my mortal enimies, if they speak not contrary to the truth & reason, must needs confess to be just and convenient.

Besides to confirm your Ma^{ty's} opinion of my innocency herein, your self may best remember how I might have departed long before this time, if I had been guilty of any crime, & that I have stood to ye uttermost trial & examination of all my dealings tho' I have tasted all times since my last restraint your Ma^{ty's} hard opinion & publick disgrace both dayly & hourly without any hope or likelyhood of ever recovering your former good opinion ; and if my protestation, who never told your majesty any untruth, may carry any credit in your opinion ; I here call God & his Angels to witness, that I would not have taken this Course if I might have stay'd in England without danger of my Soul and peril of my life. Wherefore as it is the true token of a noble mind, & hath alwayes been noted as a certain argument of your Mat^{ies} gratious disposition, in that it hath ever pleased you to take pity on those which are in misery, & to respect with the eyes of your favour all afflicted persons, so cannot I be brought any whitt to fear your Ma^{ty} will make me the first example of your severe & rigorous dealing, in laying your displeasure upon me who am inforced to forsake my Country, to forget my friends, to leave my living, & to lose ye hope of all worldly pleasures & earthly Commodities, if either I will not consent to the certain destruction of my body, or willingly yeild to ye manifest endangering of my Soul. The least of which are so intollerable for any Christian man to endure, as I hope it cannot be thought any undutifullness in me if I seek by any good & lawfull means to avoid so great an inconvenience. And tho' the loss of temporal commodities be so grievous to flesh & blood, as I could not desire to live if I were not comforted with the remembrance of his mercy, for whom I endure all this, who endured ten thousand times more for me. Yet I ensure your Ma^{ty} that your displeasure should be more unpleasant unto me than the bitterness of all my other losses, and a greater grief than my greatest misfortunes are besides.

Therefore remaining in assured hope that my self, and my Cause shall receive that favour, conceit & rightfull constructions at your majesties hands, which I may justly challenge, both because the trial of my good dealings heretofore have sufficiently deserved the same & also for y^t the Confession of my mortal enimies at this time must needs acknowledge mine innocency herein. I do humbly crave pardon for my long & tedious letter, wch the weightiness of the matter enforced me unto, & I beseech God from the bottom of my heart to send your Majesty as great happiness as I wish to mine own Soul.

CHAPTER VIII

His taking at sea, and committment to the Tower

THE Earl having writ this letter, & provided all necessaries for his Journey caused a ship secretly to be hired, in which he intended to have gon from some private port in Sussex or Hamshire, & he took only two servants to attend upon him, Mr William Bray & Mr Burlace. He went towards the place where the ship lay two several times to have embarked himself, & was forced to return back, because the winds were so contrary, that the ship could not get out of the harbor, at the least it was so signified to him. But more probable it is, that was but an excuse framed by the master of the ship or some other by whom he was betrayed to cause delay until all things were in readiness for his takeing at Sea & bringing back again : because at the very time, as was well known, other ships departed from other ports not far distant, & had both wind & weather favourable enough to carry them to Calis & other partes of France.

But at length when the Shipman did signify that the wind was fit & all in readiness, he went unto the port, embarked himself, & that night put forth to Sea ; but after a while, the Shipman having hung out a light for a Sign, he was boarded, & stayed by one Keloway Captain of a little ship of war, who pretended himself to be a Pirate, & so was thought by the Earl and his Company, because being known by them to be a man of a notorious infamous life, they had no reason, as they said, to imagine that he was employed by publick authority for the stoping and taking of them. This Keloway (or whosoever he were that took that name upon him) offered to let the Earl and his two gentlemen pass free for one hundred pounds in money, swearing he should presently without any further stop or stay from him pass safely into France if he would but write a word or two to any friend of his of whom he might receive it. Whereupon the Earl little suspecting any latent fraud wrote in few lines to his sister the Lady Margaret Sackvil that she should speak to Mr Bridges aliàs Grately a Priest, to give one hundred pound to ye bearer thereof, by the token that was betwixt them that *black, is white*, & with all assured her that now he hoped assuredly to have speedy passage without impediment. Keloway as soon as he got this letter of the Earl read it, and immediately after discovered himself that he was appointed by the Council to watch there for him, & carry him back again to land, as he did forthwith, giving notice unto them with all speed of all that he had done.

The Earl was nothing at all daunted with this so unexpected accident, & not only wth great patience and courage did endure it, but moreover carry'd it with a joyfull & merry countenance. His money & all those things he had about him, as Jewels & the like, were forthwith seased upon, & himself conducted with a strong gard towards London by Sir George Cary son & heir to the Lord Hunsden, then Chamberlain to the Queen. One night he lodged in the way at Guilford in Surrey, where seeing the master of the inne who sometime had been his servant. & some other who wished well unto him, weeping & sorrowing for his misfortune, he comforted them all, & willed them to be of good cheere, because it was not for any crime, treason or the like, as perhaps it was divulged, that he was apprehended & carry'd in y^t manner, but only for attempting to leave the Kingdome, the which he had done only for his own safety, & to free himself from the danger of his enimies the which both God & nature do allow. The day following he was carried to London, & there committed Prisoner to the tower upon the 25 of april 1585. His Brother the Lord William, & his sister the Lady Margaret were, not long after committed to several Prisons; the which when he understood was far more grief to him, as he signify'd in a letter to his Lady, than all his own trouble & imprisonment.

CHAPTER IX

His Examination & Censure in the Starr-Chamber

SOON after his committment he was twice examin'd by some of the Council who were sent unto him to the tower for that special purpose by the Queen. The first examination was upon may day, the which being ended Sir Christopher Hatton then Vice-chamberlain & of the privy council, stayed with him after the departure of the rest, and wished him if he loved his life not to conceal any of those things which were already known as that he, & his Brother the Lord William had sent to Dr Allen. That they had attempted to go over. That they had heared from, & offer'd to be directed by him. That Mr Bridges the Priest was the messenger who was commanded by Dr Allen to deliver the message unto them both jointly, and came unto them by the name of Grately with diverse other circumstances which were all most true. For Mr Bridges had out of Confidence told all these things to one Mr Gilbert Gifford a Priest who then lived at paris in france, & after was discovered to be a spye who gave intelligence of these & all other things he could come to know unto some of the Council. He told them also that one Mr Henry Dun a gentleman of his acquaintance who then was a servant to Sir Christopher Hatton, and he had confessed them all, being called as it seems in some question thereabout, as the same Sir Christopher then told the Earl out of good will, promising him if he would set it all down plainly to do his best endeavor to save him from danger. Otherwise the very denial itself would cast more danger upon him, than all his friends living would be able to save. Hereupon the Earl after many thanks for his great love & friendly counsel declared plainly every thing as it was, and the cause why he had sent to Dr Allen, clearing his brother the Ld William of all things saveing only his attempt to have gone over with him the first time he intended to have gone.

The next time that the Council came to examin him, they often asked & earnestly what he would have done beyond seas: his answer was; He would have served in any place that Doctor Allen had judged fit for him, so that it had been for the Catholick cause. They asking again if he would have done any thing against the Queen or ye State of this Realm upon Dr Allen's perswasions. He said that no, not for a world. They demanded then if the title of Duke of Norfolk had been ever offer'd him, or if Dr Allen had ever written to him by that title. He answered that never; and that one haveing said unto him that he should have a better title than he had when he came beyond seas. He presently reply'd, that he would never have better whilst he lived. They asked what cause moved him to write to Dr Allen: he answer'd that upon Master Bridges his speeches, who told him that the Earl of Leicester had vow'd to make the name of a Catholick as odious in England as the name of a Turk & therefore wished him to write to Dr Allen, that if some means might be found how to deal with that Earl, or that he might be taken away by some lawfull means, it would be a great good for ye Catholick Cause, & a great safety to all Catholicks here in England. And this he said because he doubted they had intercepted his letter to Dr Allen by Mr Dun's means, who knew where it was, & that at his departure to sea, it was not out of England.

After this they charged him with a letter that contained great danger both to the Queen & State: to which he answer'd most truly that he never heared nor knew of any such. Whereupon they shew'd him one of three sides of papar at the least, but would not suffer him to read more of it than the two first lines, which were these. *Sir, this letter containeth such matter as is fitter for the fire to consume, than to be laid up in your study.* In it was written (as partly he then perceived by ye Examiners) but better afterwards by other means) that tho' he went away poorly, he should return in glory, & land in Norfolk with a great power of men to trouble both the Queen & State. It was written in a hand resembling his very much unto Mr William Dix his principal Officer, a man of good estate in Norfolk, & to make it more colourable, it mentioned diverse particular matters both touching sales of wood which he had made, & others which he would have made. The Council told him he should be arraigned about y^t letter. His answer was that if there were no remedy but that he must needs die, he beseeched God to have mercy on his soul, & desired their Lordships to become humble sutors to the queen in his behalf that he might not be called in question of his life for that of which he was never guilty; but as innocent both from that & all kind of treason, as the child now newly born. That letter doubtlesse was forged by some of his enimies who intended to have thereby procured his death and destruction. It was first brought to light, as he understood afterwards, by Sir Francis Walsingham the queen's secretary a heavy friend of his, or by some of his instruments, & was pretended to have been intercepted at the very time of his going to sea; by which it was apparent to have been forged by some who had notice beforehand of his going, as the Secretary & some others of his greatest enimies had, even from the beginning. But most of the Council could never be ascertain'd either where or how it was taken: for which respect the best of them did esteem of it no otherwise than a forged thing, as indeed it evidently appeared to be by some things contain'd in it, which shewed that the writer had in truth smal knowledge or acquaintance with the Earls affaires. And therefore they neither thought it convenient ever to arraign him thereupon as some of them had threaten'd; nor when he was brought into the Starr-chamber (which was done not long after) where all that could be alledged against him was manifested to the world & exaggerated to the utmost, this letter for any thing I could ever learn, was never mention'd.

The principal points alledged against him there, were his attempting to have left the Realm without licence of the Queen. His being reconciled to the Church of Rome. Together with a certain writing of his servant Burlacy, who was one of those who was to have gone with him, wherein something was contein'd about his being to be made Duke of Norfolk. To which last he protested that Burlacy never acquainted him with any such thing, & that he never so much as heared thereof until the present time wherein they alledged it against him. His writing to, and intelligence with Dr Allen was brought against him. But as for his being reconciled, he acknowledged that he had confessed his Sins to a Priest, & had been absolved by him from them, the which he said, that all might know he was a Catholick: but that in any other manner he was not reconciled. Concerning his writing to Dr Allen,

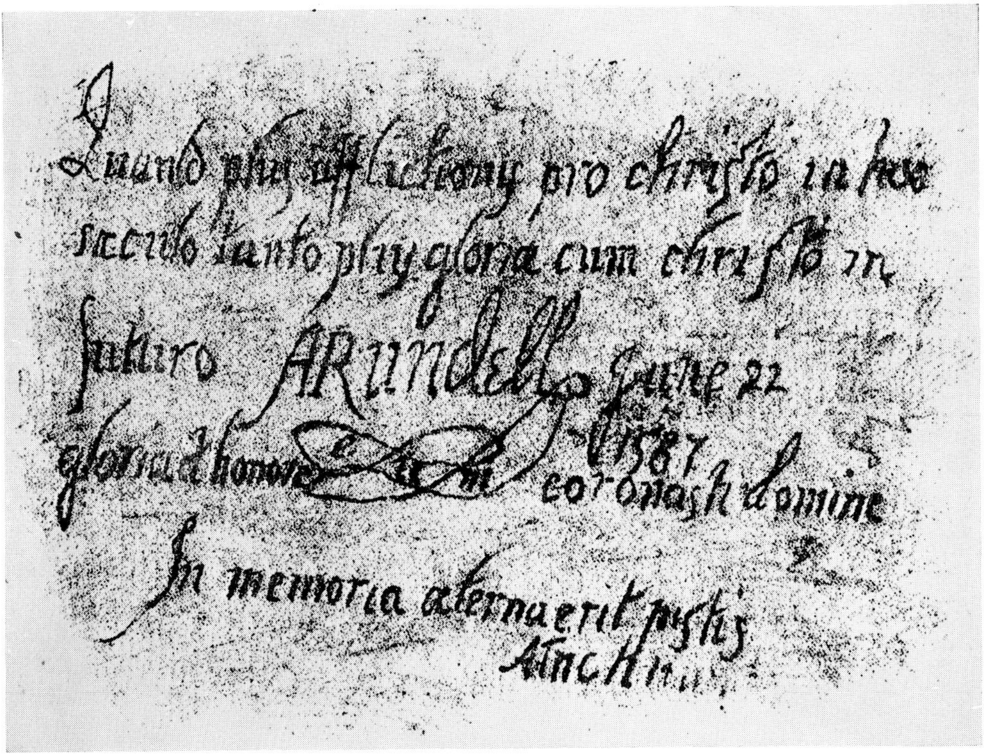

PLATE I

Inscription carved by St. Philip Howard over the fireplace in the
Beauchamp Tower, Tower of London

Quanto plus afflictionis pro christo in hoc sæculo tanto plus gloriæ cum christo in futuro.
Arundell June 22 1587 (The more affliction for Christ in this world, so much the more glory
with Christ in the future)

Thomas Howard, 4th Duke of Norfolk, 1537/8 – 1572
Father of St. Philip Howard

PLATE III

Mary, Duchess of Norfolk, 1540 – 1557
Mother of St. Philip Howard

Signatures of some Elizabethan statesmen including Henry FitzAlan,
Earl of Arundel, 1512 – 1579/80, Grandfather of St. Philip Howard

See page 82 for a transcript of this document

he answered as he had done before unto the Council when they examined him thereof. And for his attempting to leave the Kingdome, he alledged the reasons which he had set down in his letter to the queen & were well known to the Council & many more, because Mr Bridges soon after his taking & apprehension had publish'd it among the Catholicks, tho' without any Order from him, yea utterly against his mind. Finally he gave such sufficient answers to every thing that was objected against him, & behaved himself so discreetly, with such chearfullness and alacrity that he got that day much credit & reputation both to his person & cause, tho' he were then fined by that Court in 10000 pounds unto the Queen, and adjudged to imprisonment during her pleasure, which continued even till his dying day, ten years & more after the sentence given.

CHAPTER X

The Strictnes of his imprisonment,
And hard usage therein

As his imprisonment was no less long and tedious, than even now I signify'd in the precedent Chapter, so was it also for the most part of that time very strict. For besides the lieutenant of the Tower who had charge over him, there was ever some gentleman of good sort specially appointed by the queen to be his Keeper; by whom he was so narrowly looked to, that for several years he could not speak with any person whatsoever but in his presence & hearing. During ye first 13 months after his committment, that is from april 1585, till the end of may 1586 he had no servants of his own to attend upon him, & never came out of his chamber to walk in any other room or take the air a little in the garden, but either his Keeper or the Lieutenant, or both of them were ever present with him. After that time he was permitted to have sometimes one, sometimes two of his own servants to be with him, but with such condition, that after their entrance there, they remained as prisoners, and neither could depart thence without special leave of the Council, nor so much as walk into the garden, or into any other room besides their Lords lodgings, but at such times & with such persons, as it pleased the Keeper to appoint, and all the rest of the night and day they were lock'd up, & could not speak with any body living. In which respect, as also by reason of the uncomfortableness of the room wherein they & their Lord were lock'd up, as having no sight of the Sun for the greatest part of the year, together with the noisomness thereof caused by a vault that was near or under it, which at some times did smell so ill, that the Keeper could scarce endure to enter into it, much less to stay there any time. For these respects, I say, there was none of his servants but were long weary of being with him there, before they could obtain licence to be dismiss'd, and some of them were kept there untill through weakness and indisposition caused by being kept so close, they were not able to do him almost any service, at least not such as his necessities did require, he being very often troubled with diverse sicknesses & diseases, which were occasioned for the most part by his so great restraint & strict imprisonment, as some learned Physitians who best knew the state of his body did affirm.

But neither were his infirmities and indispositions tho' many & great; nor his imprisonment tho' long & strict, so grievous & troublesome unto him as some other things he there endured. As first; the hard & harsh dealing of the Lieutenant, who, as I have heared both from his Lady & others, did all he could to afflict and vex him. The Earl himself in a letter which he wrote to a certain friend of his something more than a year before his death, did signify it in this manner. His injuries (towit the Lieutenant) to me both by himself & his trusty Roger are intollerable, infinite, dayly multiply'd, & to those who know them not, incredible: and the most that you can imagin, will be far inferior, I think, to the truth when you shall hear it. Secondly; the bad disposition of some of his Keepers, who besides their strictness towards him went about to intrap him, had he not been very wary & circumspect, & did sometimes report things of him, that not only were wholy fals, but might have been, & perhaps were of great prejudice unto him. As that he never spoke one good word of the queen, when as in all occasions he spoke with great respect of her, & protested many times in their presence & hearing, that he was alwayes ready to do any lawfull thing that lay in his power to do her service & give her contentment. One of those his Keepers who made great shew of friendship unto him would often take occasion to ask him what he would do if the Pope should excommunicate the Queen, or make any war against her: and if he were silent therein, or passed it away by talking of other matters without answering directly to those questions, yet professing all loyalty & duty to the queen, most commonly he would send his man the next day with letters to the Court, as the Earl himself did observe, who tho' he would not directly judge, yet he could not but fear there was no good meaning nor dealing therein.

CHAPTER XI

Other injuries & calumnies during his Imprisonment

BESIDES the injuries received from his Keepers & the Lieutenant of the Tower, the ingratitude & treachery of some who had been his servants in former times & had received great benefits from him, together with the unkind dealing of some who were very near in blood unto him was no smal occasion of affliction to his mind. For whereas the Duke his Father had made such a kind of conveyance of the greatest part of his Estate that it could not be forfeited by attainder, as de facto it was not by his own, but came all safely to the Earl his Son, some who knew the particulars of his Estate better than others as haveing been employ'd in his affaires, did not only upon his attainder treacherously discover all they could to his detriment, but moreover prosecuted the suit in the queens behalf in such manner against him, that a good part of his lands was thereby lost which otherwise had been saved. His own brother also the Lord Thomas Howard made meanes unto the queen immediately upon his attainder for the obtaining to his own use & behoof of diverse Lordships belonging unto him, the which some others who were strangers unto him (as in particular Sir Christopher Hatton) out of friendship & honourable respect would not accept of, when they were offered unto them by the queen her self without any motion at all from themselves.

Another of his afflictions proceeded from the malice of some about the Court who did their utmost endeavour not only to incense the queen against him, to defame & disgrace him with the world but also to have wrought his death, ruin, & destruction. They possessed the queen that he made himself a Catholick, or rather made shew to be such an one, not out of any Religion, but only to oppose himself to her & shew a dislike of her government

& proceedings : His Lady at the beginning of his troubles, going unto the queen to sue for him, was rated exceedingly by Sir Francis Knowles then privy Counellour,[1] asking her if she & her husband were not ashamed to make themselves Papists only out of spleen & peevish humour to cross, & vex the queen. The like they endeavoured to have perswaded the world of him, publishing y^t he was of no Religion, & to make it more probable, they brought one who in publick Court at Westminster took a solemn oath that he heared a Catholick Priest say, that the Earl of Arundel had so smal regard of Religion that he would not stick to hear *Masse in the Morning*, & go in the *afternoon to a Protestant Sermon*. And this Calumnie was so divulged, that some of his Keepers told him, how very many in ye Kingdome were of opinion that he made shew to be a Catholick only out of Policy : to whom with great mildness he made this answer. "That God alone doth know the Secrets of mens hearts, "&, that he thought there was smal policy for a man to lose his "liberty, hazard his estate and life, & live in that manner in "a prison as he then did.

To move the queen moreover against him and make him be abridged of the little liberty which after much suite he had obtained of the Council to go out of his own lodging in the company of his Keeper to walk sometimes a little in a Certain Gallery within the Tower, they informed her, that many Caps & Knees, & Courtesies were made unto him, when he stood in the gallery window : which was so wholy fals as he protested in a Letter to the Ld Chancellor, that he neither ever saluted any one, nor any one made the least shew towards him in that place : but that it was true that walking one day in the Garden with his Keeper, one from the leads of the Salttower saluted him with a very low reverence. whereat he marvail'd & desired his Keeper to talk with him, who had the Custody of that tower and to charge him that he might no more be so abused. Yet four or five dayes after the same man, in the same place not contented with an ordinary salutation or reverence, bowed himself so low, that his head was within a foot of the ground, & then lifting up his hands he remain'd in that posture looking directly in the Earl's and his Keeper's face whilst they walked the whole length of the alley. The which they seeing and being troubled thereat, to avoid it they presently went into the other part of the

---

[1] sic

garden. But immediately the man removed himself also to the other side of the leads which was nearest to the place where they were, & there used the like ceremonies as before. Which made the Earl think that either the man was mad or set there of purpose to mock him, or for a ground to raise that report which was made to the queen of his being saluted with Caps & Courtesies for the hindering y^t little liberty he had obtain'd of the Council.

And not without cause he might suspect it was done on set purpose to molest & abuse him, seeing by experience he found far greater & worse things to have been done of set purpose against him. For besides the forging the letter above mentioned, which was before his comeing into ye tower; after his comeing thither they slandered him first; with incontinency, as tho' he had there got a woman with child, & suborned a base dishonest baggage servant to one Mr Pigeon dwelling in the Tower, to lay her child to his charge: and sent a certain catholick gentlewoman (Mrs Albridge afterwards marryed to Dr Lodge) with whome I was acquainted and whose husband was a dependent of Sir Francis Walsingham then Secretary, & had been his Spye at Rome & other places diverse years, to give notice to his Lady thereof upon pretence she might take some secret order for the maintenance of the woman & the childe, lest otherwise the matter might come to light, & her Lord be disgraced. But she out of the assurance of his innocency therein, & surmising it to be some plot of his enimies, as indeed it was, to disgrace him and afflict her, gave such answer to the gentlewoman whose simplicity was abused therein, that she remained much ashamed to have been so over credulous in such a business which upon a little examination appeared not only improbable, but altogether impossible, considering both the strict imprisonment of the Earl, he never going out of his chamber without either his Keeper or the Lieutenant, or both of them with him, nor any comeing into it but in their presence, & with their consent. As also his sickness & infirmity at the very time when it was said that the child shou'd be begotten. Besides he had been so wickedly disposed he never would have made choice (as himself did say) of one so base, so old, & so ugly as she was. Yet to make the matter seem more credible, the inventors thereof added diverse circumstances thereto: as that the Earl had first made her a

Catholick, had given her great Summes of money, & that she came to him apparrell'd in a gown of green tafity.

But this calumny not succeeding, as being too palpable a falsity, they went about to defame him of intemperance in drinking, a vice from which he was exceeding far, as all those who waited on him did ever testifie : for that betwixt his meals he never used to drink at all, and at his meals was alwayes very moderate. All ye ground they had for the raising this report was that he used for a time to drink thrice a week a little metheglin in the morning partly to comfort his stomach being weak, partly to be freed from costiveness to which he was much subject. Divers other such like slanders they raised of him at several times, & they were so many, that himself in a letter to a friend did say, it seemed to him they rose as Hydra's heads, no sooner one did fall, but more still were raised in room thereof. And so many gins were dayly laid to intrapp him, that had he not been very wary & circumspect he had been brought into very great danger oftentimes.

CHAPTER XII

The means & manner how he was intrap'd

THOUGH his waryness was very great to keep himself from either doing or saying any thing that might be occasion of any danger to him, yet was he at length brought into it by means of some Catholicks then prisoners in the tower, whose weakness was therein abused by his enimies. These were Sir Thomas Gerard a Knight of good worth in Lancashire : one Mr. Shelly a Sussex gentleman, and Mr. William Bennet an old priest of Queen Mary's dayes, who having been conformable for a time unto queen Elizabeth's proceedings, because afterwards he was reconciled again to the Catholick Church, he so much thereby incurred the displeasure of the State, that he was therefore committed prisoner to the Tower, where he was placed in a chamber not far from the lodgings of the Earl, who having at that time, which was about ye beginning of the year 1588 and three years after his commitment, much more liberty than ever he had either before or after, and desiring to meet & speak with him for the comfort of his own soul, found means to bring it to effect by mediation of the Lieutenants daughter who had thirty pound given her by the Earl's Lady (as herself told me) for her endeavour in procuring it. This being first obtain'd, he used such diligence afterwards that he got also churchstuff & all things requisit for the celebration of the holy Sacrifice of the Mass whereto himself did serve with great humility, & therein receiv'd the blessed Sacrament frequently as long as that liberty did last ; during which time he met also wth Sir Thomas Gerard both at Mass & at other times, as also with Mr Shelly tho' not so frequently.

Much discours there was about that time of the great Spanish fleet which was then in preparation, whereupon it happened that the Earl in his discourses with them did manifest sometimes much affection to the King of Spain, not only in regard of the obligation & duty he bore unto him as being his Godfather ; but also because in those times & for diverse years he was the chief maintainer & defender of the Catholick Religion. And in respect there went then a rumor very currant amonsgt ye Catholicks about London, that a suddain massacre of them all was intended upon the first landing of the Spaniards, & this comeing to the Earl's ear, out of his piety he judged it necessary that all Catholicks should forthwith apply themselves to prayer either for the avoiding of that danger, or for the better preparing themselves thereto. And to the end it might be done more orderly & efficaciously, he both persuaded the above mentioned with whom he spoke to make prayer for four and twenty hours togather for that end, & also sent to some others to the same purpose, whereof one of greater prudence & experience than the rest signify'd unto him that perhaps it might be otherwise interpreted by the State, than he intended, wishing him therefore to desist; as presently thereupon he did, but when it was too late. For some of his enimies having got intelligence thereof, took occasion to conceive all that prayer to be made & meant by him for the good Success of the Spanish fleet, and afterwards induced both Mr Shelly & Sir Thomas Gerard either through fear or fair promises to testifie the same against him, as also Mr Bennet to confess how he had entreated him to say a Mass of the Holy Ghost to the same effect.

CHAPTER XIII

His Examination about that Business

AFTER the fear of the Spanish fleet was well passed, towards the end of the year 88, the Earl was again committed to close custody, and twice examin'd by some of the Council who were purposely sent by the queen for that end to ye tower. The first time was by Sir Christopher Hatton then Ld Chancellor, Sir William Cecil Ld Treasurer, and Sir Thomas Hennage who had ever been a great enimy of his. They examin'd him first about his desireing Mr Bennet to say Mass for the success of the Spaniards, & of making the prayer of 24 hours to the same end: to both which he answer'd negatively. That he should have said, how the Catholicks e'er long would plague the protestants as well as they had been plagued by them. To which he said he hoped their Lordships did not think him of so bad a conscience as to go with such a mind to Mass, & to receive the blessed Sacrament as he usually did then. Lastly they charged him with burning certain papers at Masse time, which they affirmed to contain matter of great importance & intelligence, & moreover that he determined to get the strongest place in the Tower for his defence against the comeing of the Spaniards. To both which he answered so fully, that they were never after alledged against him, neither at his arraignment, nor in his Second examination. For the papers contained nothing as he protested but his confession, & matters concerning his conscience: & to ye other, that because it was said a massacre was intended to be made of them, he seemed to approve Sir Thomas Gerard's proposition, who told him that ye lodgings where he lay were the best for their defence, as having in them some gunstones, & other weapons wch he shewed him.

For his second examination besides those three which came before, the Lord Hunsdon was also sent by the queen. And therein after the three first points objected in his first examination, they added that he should say, *Cardinal Allen had the disposition of the Crown*; whereto the party to whom it was spoken should answer *that was a purple word*. To all wch he having answered negatively, immediately Mr Bennet & Sir Thomas Gerard were brought forth to affirm before his face, that of the Mass & 24 hours of prayer, but he was enjoin'd not to speak at all, nor make any answer unto them. The which was done as he conceived & signified to a friend, only to embolden them against the time they should come to ye bar against him. After their departure he was bid to say what he would; but because he judged that offer to be made only out of policy to know his answers before hand, that so his accusers & adversaries might be the better prepared to make reply thereto against the time of his arraignment, therefore he contain'd himself, & made no answer at all.

Whereupon the Lord Treasurer abruptly asked him whether he would hold him for a traitor who should say that the Pope had any authority to deprive the queen. His answer was, that he never heared any say so, & when he did his Lordship should hear what he would say. The treasurer urged him twice or thrice to answer Categoricè: the like was done by the Lord Chamberlain: to whom he said that he wonder'd, he should be asked such questions, seeing he was accused of no such matter, & both had been, & was at all times ready to serve the queen with his life and goods against any Prince or Potentate whatsoever: to which the Lord Chamberlain replyed. What against the Pope? he answer'd by asking whether the Pope was not included within the name of a forreign prince or potentate? And as he signify'd in a letter to a friend, tho' he knew he might safely have answer'd affirmatively to y^t question, yet because he saw them determined to take his life, as he then thought, & knew not how they would misreport his words, for fear of giveing scandal he would not answer directly. Then one of the Examiners said the *Pope was an errant knave*, another called him *Pild Italian Priest*. & the Lord Chamberlan entring into passion called the Earl beast & traytor, & said rather than he should not be hanged within four dayes, that he himself would hang him, repeating it once or twice. To which the Earl answered, the sooner the better if it please God. The which he said that the Chamberlain might know he feared not his threats. & when as the said Lord

Chancellor urged him to set down under his hand that he would not answer to that question of the Pope's power to depose ye queen he flatly denyed to do it, as being a thing no way belonging or pertaining to him. The Treasurer who said it was no marvell he was so settled in religion, because he did read nothing to the contrary. He answered resolutely, that he neither did nor would do by his Lordship's favour. And therewith they all rose, left him & went their way.

CHAPTER XIV

His Arraignment and Condemnation

NOT long after these examinations he was brought from the tower to the Kings bench Court in the hall of Westminster, & there publickly arraigned about the aforesaid points upon the 14 day of April 1589. Yet in the mean time it so happened that Mr Bennet the Priest who was one of his accusers, being removed from the tower, & prisoner at that time in the Counter of Woodstreet in London haveing remorse of conscience for what he had already done, writ this following letter to him, & by means of a Catholick then prisoner in the same Counter, got it sent to his Lady. The Superscription was in this manner: To the right honourable the Earl of Arundel be these delivered. the letter thus.

Right honourable & most Noble Peer.

I most humbly upon my Knees before God & all his Angels, & before all the world, if need require, wth a most penitent, rent, & afflicted conscience and heart, crave mercy & forgiveness for the great offence I have committed against your honour in my last troubles and confessions. So it is Right honourable, that being called in question about certain supposed offences in the tower, unto which my answer not being to their contentment, a letter of mine own hand, which I writ to a Priest there in defence of my Jurisdiction by him brought in question, was produced; and because therein I derived my authority from the See Apostolick, I was accounted & term'd as a dead man amongst them without her Majestie's Special pardon which was promised upon condition &c *Pauca Sapienti*. with many fair promises & allurements togather with many thundering threats of returning to tower, torments & death it self, If I failed. Which unexpected letter of mine, with threats mingled wth promise of life & speedy liberty, togather with the great weakness both of body & mind by reason of my long & sore imprisonment, I was stroken into such an astonishment & maze, that I confess'd every thing that seemed to content their humour, which I perceived not at the first altogether to tend to the ruin of your Honour. But being demanded whether you did send a note to the Priests in Coleharbor to pray for the good success of the Spanish fleet, I answered, as truth was, that I never knew, or was privy to any such note: yet with a guilty, fearfull unjust & most tormented conscience only for saveing of my life & liberty, I confessed that you moved me to say a Mass of the Holy Ghost for the good success of the Spanish fleet. For which unjust confession, or rather accusation I do again & again, & so to my life's end most instantly crave Gods pardon & yours, and for my better satisfaction of this my unjust suggestion I will if need require, offer up both life & limbs in averring my accusation to be, as it is indeed, & as I shall answer before Almighty God, before the face of Angels & men, most unjust, & done only of fear of the Tower, torments, & death. Thus not doubting of your Honour's gratious pardon & forgiveness, I will rest my poor afflicted conscience in only Gods mercy. My body & life I freely offer to the world to dispose as it shall please God. The Holy Trinity preserve your Honour from Peril of soul & body.   Amen.

 Your Honours poor Beadsman
  WILLIAM BENNET Priest.

This letter was inclosed & fast sealed in another of a different hand without name or date, endorsed thus: To the Right Honourable the Countess of Arundel these be dd. The contents as followeth. My Duty, (Right honourable & very good Lady) considered; these are to advertise your Ladyship, that whereas My lord your husband hath been wrongfully accused by one who hartily repenting himself thereof, hath here, as I take it, both acknowledged this fault, & craved pardon for the same. I thought it a part of Christian Charity (though I am utterly unknown both to your Lord & yourself) to convey them to your Honour close seal'd, hoping they will be some testimony of your husband's innocency. Charging your Honour as you will answer at the dreadfull day of judgment (pardon me good Madam I beseech you) not to accept of them, except you resolve never to shew them till your said husband come in question. And thus hoping to find that expectation of honour & vertue which is esteem'd to be in your Honour, I do most humbly take my leave, committing your Honour to God's merciful tuition.

At the Earl's Arraignment both Sir Thomas Gerard & Mr Bennet were brought in person to give witness against him: the one that he required a Mass of the Holy Ghost to be said for the success of the Spaniards: the other that the prayer of 24 hours was directed to the same end. Both which he deny'd very stout & constantly, pleading the above-mention'd letter of Mr Bennet against his testification in such manner that he not being able to deny it, some of the Lords there present told him he was a fals man & no lawful witness. Many other things were objected & exaggerated against him by the queen's Council, to all which he answer'd so resolute & readily, that most there present were of opinion he would have been acquitted by the Noblemen his Peers, but it proved far otherwise. For he was condemned of high treason, & accordingly had sentence then pronounced against him: the which he heared not only without being daunted therewith any thing at all, but shewing moreover such a chearfullness in his looks, as well witnessed the inward innocency & quiet of his mind.

CHAPTER XV

What he did after his Condemnation

THE day after his condemnation he writ, & sent this ensuing letter to the Ld Chancellor. My special good Lord. I am most hartily sorry that I was so hastily[1] prevented by my hasty departure from the Bar, presently after the sentence pronounced upon me, as I wanted time to make humble suite for her Majesty's favour. And I am very glad that I have this oportunity of writing to your Lordship to make humble petition unto her majesty in my behalf for her gratious favour together with my most harty grief for any thing whereinsoever I have offended her highness in all ye course of my life. As also to give your L^{d}ship humble thanks for your honourable goodness always extended towards me, & to become a most earnest suiter for the continuance thereof to my wife & children. And as a dead man to this world, & in all good will whilst I live, your Lordships most affectionate I humbly take my leave, beseeching God to send you all honour & happiness in this world to his glory, & my poor soul a joyfull meeting with yours in heaven. The day after my condemnation.

    Your L^{d}ship's most humbly
      at commandment till my last
          PHILIPP HOWARD.

But in another letter to Father Southwell he declared that his meaning in those words of the precedent letter wherein he acknowledged a hearty grief for having offended the queen, was not for any of those things whereof he had been arraign'd, but in respect he had so long time waited upon her, it could not be, but that he had offended her many wayes in the cours of his life, & being then desireous to ask pardon of the meanest person living thereby to be

---

[1] This word has been deleted in the manuscript.

the better prepared for death which he dayly expected; much more he thought it convenient to do the same of the queen. And so much he declared also to the gentleman who then was his keeper; adding withall that he would never make submission, or crave pardon of any thing whereof he was arraigned, considering he had committed no fault therein, & therefore would never bely himself. To the same effect he writ then also a letter to the queen herself with protestation of his innocency; the which yet was not delivered, by reason the Ld Chancellor was of opinion it would rather incense her against him, than otherwise. He resolved moreover if he should be put to death for that cause, publickly to declare himself innocent & faultless therein: And because Catholicks were not sometimes permitted then to speak any thing for the clearing of themselves, he therefore provided a writing by which he declared his mind, & thereof writ diverse copies both in English & Latin with his own hand & subscribed with his name, intending at his execution to cast them amongst the people, in case he were not permitted to speak. The form of them was as follows.

Seeing Almighty God hath vouchsafed of his infinit goodness to call me being the meanest of all his servants, & most unworthy, I must confess, of so great honour to bear witness of the Catholick Faith, & Roman church, I thought it fit, for preventing of all sinister practices, which might be used either to the disgrace of my faith or discredit of my self to testify that under my hand, in as effectual manner, as I could, which I am ready to seal with my blood, by the grace & assistance of our Lord, whensoever need & occasion shall require: that neither the innocency of my mind, nor integrity of mine actions may be defaced by the untrue suggestions of others (as to men in my state it often happens) nor my firm resolution in the Catholick & Roman Faith perverted by the false reports of evill disposed persons. For albeit I must acknowledge my self most frail, & a heinous sinner, yet as I am bound to maintain in my self the name & faith of a Catholick man (which next unto God I hold in greatest price & account, & which every faithfull Christian ought to esteem above all other things whatsoever) so do I most desire that all men should take me for such an one, as in truth I am, & that no man should be either mislead or beguiled by malicious & untrue reports to think otherwise of me, than both my words & deeds do plainly testifie. Wherefore for the satisfaction of all men, & discharge of my conscience before God, I here protest before his Divine Majesty & all the Holy Court of heaven, that I have committed no treason, & that the Catholick & Roman Faith which I hold, is the only cause (as far as I can any way imagin) why either I have been thus long imprisoned, or for which I am now ready to be executed. And I do most firmly, resolutely and unmoveably hold & believe this One, Holy, Catholick, and Apostolick Faith. And as I will die in ye same so am I most ready at all times, if need be, to yield my life for defence thereof. And whatsoever ye most Sacred Council of Trent hath established touching faith & manners, I believe & hold. And whatsoever it hath condemned, I condemn in my soul, & renounce here under my hand, & abjure from the bottom of my heart. And I do most earnestly desire, that all Catholicks conceive this opinion of me, & take me so, as I have here protested myself to be, & not credit any untrue reports that have, may, or shall be spread of me to the contrary: for as Christ is life unto me, so account I death a most happy & glorious gain unto me being in defence of his faith, & for his holy name. And thus I will conclude with beseeching almighty God the Father of mercies, & God of all consolation to grant peace unto his Church, Charity & grace to mine enimies, Salvation & felicity to the queen, & realm, & to me as an untimely fruit (being born before my time) & the meanest of all his Servants a constant perseverance in his holy faith and the love of his Divine Majesty. Amen. By me a most humble & obedient child of the Catholick Roman Church.

Philipp Howard

The same in substance which is contain'd in this writing he told unto the gentleman his keeper, as himself signify'd in a private letter to F^r Southwel which I have seen: to wit, that at his death he would protest, he died only for Religion, and was wholy guiltless of any true crime against the queen. And when the gentleman told him: But if some ask you then of particulars, whether you had required a Mass to be said for the good success of the Spaniards &c. what will you say? his answer was this. Marry deny it as I did in my examination and arraignment. The gentleman replying that he thought a man at that time would speak as afore God. He answer'd that a man who fears God would do the same in any place, & since I deny'd, saith he, in a place of open Justice, you have no cause to doubt that I will deny it at my death, & that I did it not. The gentleman perceiving thereby his determination gave notice thereof unto the Lord Chamberlain & some others of the Council, who thereupon as it should seem, perswaded the queen that he might not be put to Death, with whom some also that were well affected towards him (as the Chancellor & Treasurer) did concurr, contrary to ye mind & desire of others who were his enimies. But whether it were upon the advice of those Councellors, or some other respect different from the abovementioned that the queen defer'd his execution, and in the end resolved to spare his life, yet it was not notified unto him of a long time, rather ye contrary was diverse times insinuated ; whereby it came to pass that he was in a continual expectation of death & making preparation for it very carefully diverse years. For tho' he lived very regularly ever after his committment to the Tower, & spent much time every day in prayer & devotion, yet more after his condemnation than before, as well will appear by that, I shall set down in the chapter following of the course and order he used to observe therein.

CHAPTER XVI

The manner of his life in ye Tower

IN the beginning when he was first committed to the Tower, he spent two hours or thereabouts every morning at his prayers. One hour & a half in the afternoons, & one quarter before he went to bed in the examination of his conscience, & recommendation of himself to Almighty God. And after some time he adjoined to his other devotions The saying of the Priestly Office, & thereby was of force something longer at prayer than before, which pious custome he continued untill the Physicians by reason of his weakness some smal time before his death compell'd him to leave it of. But after his condemnation he spent betwixt four and five hours every morning in prayer & meditation & betwixt three & four, in the afternoon. The rest of his time excepting that little he spent in walking or some other corporal exercise appointed by the Physicians, he bestowed either in writing or translating books of Piety. One Book of Lanspergius containing an Epistle of Jesus Christ to ye faithfull soul he translated out of Latin into English, & caused it to be printed for the furtherance of devotion. He writ also three treatises of the excellency & utility of vertue which never came to light by reason he was forced to send them away upon fear of a search before they were fully perfected & polished. He used to read the Spiritual books of Father Louis de Granada very frequently; & at other times the works of S. Jerome, & other Ancient Fathers; as also old Historiagraphers, particularly Eusebius, in which, as he signify'd unto F^r Southwel, he found exceeding comfort for the confirmation of his Faith by beholding there how the Church was in her Infancy. Upon Sundays & Feasts he used to read some part of the Holy Scriptures with special reverence & humility.

In the year 1588. soon after his second committment to close prison, he began to fast three days every week, mundays, wednesdays & fridays, and in them neither flesh nor fish. But finding by experience that his body was not able to endure so much, he altered it in this manner. That his one meal on mundays was of flesh : On wednesdays of fish : On fridays of neither flesh nor fish, & abstaining also from all whitmeats & wine. And this manner he observed constantly both before & after his arraignment (excepting only the wednesday immediately following it, wherein he did eat some smal thing for Supper having then some special need thereof) untill he was prescribed by his Physicians to alter that course, which was not long before his death. Many times he used also the same abstinence upon thursdays as upon mundays with only one meal of flesh. And upon some special dayes he abstained wholy from all kind of sustenance either meat or drink. These were the Vigils of the Feasts of Corpus Christi, of the Ascension of our Saviour, of all Saints, as also the Eves of the Feasts of the B^d Virgin, to whom he was particularly devout. Yet he carry'd it in such manner that none ever had any knowledg thereof, excepting one gentleman his servant, from whom I had it, whose help he used therein. For upon those dayes as soon as his dinner was brought in, the rest both of his own & the Lieutenant's servants being sent out, & the dore fast shut, he made him eat and drink the same quantity that himself usually did on other fasting dayes, which being done, and the door open again, the other servants came in to take away as at other times without ever perceiving any thing at all, by reason they saw his trenchers & napkin folded, & as much meat eaten as on other dayes.

His hour of rising in the morning was constantly at five of the clock having to that end a Larum in his chamber, & was very carefull that it should be set overnight. Immediatly as soon as he was risen out of bed, he fell down upon his bare knees, & breath'd forth in secret his first devotions to Almighty God, his eyes and hands lifted up to heaven with his kneeling in that manner then and at other times, his knees were grown very hard and black. While he made him self ready (wherein he spent but little time) he used some vocal prayers wherein he was so unwilling to be interrupted, that if it happen'd any of his servants to have spoken but a word unto him in that time, he would make no answer at all, till he had ended, and then would tell them how great a displeasure therein they did unto him, warning them withall to do the like no more. All the following hours of yᵉ day were very orderly distributed by him into a certain and set manner, some to one exercise, some to another; but the most, as I said before, to prayer and practice of devotion. And always at nine at night, except upon some extraordinary occasion, after the examination of his conscience, he betook himself to his rest. In those times which were allotted to walking or other recreation, his discourse and conversation either with his Keeper, or the Lieutenant, or his own servants was either tending to Piety, or some profitable discourse, as of the lives and examples of holy men, of the sufferances and constancy of the Martyrs of ancient times, from which he would usually deduce some good document or other: as of the facility of a vertuous life after a man had once overcome his sensuality; of the happiness of those that suffer'd any thing for our Saviour's sake with such like: to which purpose he had writ with his own hand upon the wall of his chamber this Latin sentence: quanto plus afflictionis pro Christo in hoc sæculo, tanto plus gloriæ cum Christo in futuro. The more affliction we endure for Christ in this world, the more glory we shall obtain with Christ in yᵉ next. The which he used often to shew to his servants as well to animate himself to suffer all his afflictions with patience & alacrity, as to incite them also to do the same.

CHAPTER XVII

The occasion of his last Sickness, and manner of his Death

AFTER he had lived diverse years in this vertuous and pious manner to the great edification of all, and admiration of such as had known the exceeding liberty wherein he lived while he was a Protestant: It happen'd that in the month of August of the year 1595, he fell one day sitting at dinner so very ill immediatly upon the eating of a roasted teal that he was forced to rise from table, and after some vehement casting he entred into a dissentery which could never be stay'd till his very death, which gave occasion unto many to suspect he was poisoned. Whereupon the Countess his wife forthwith sent him some antidotes and all the remedies she could any way procure: but all in vain. For the disease had so possessed him that it could not be removed, but by little & little so consumed his body that he became like an anatomy haveing nothing left but skin and bone. Some were of opinion that the poison was put by his cook into the sauce of the roasted teal being thereto corrupted by one Nicolas Rainberde who sometime had been the Earl's servant, and after was employ'd by the Queen against him prosecuting sundry suits in ye Exchequer to overthrow his Estate, wherein when he perceived he could not prevail, and fearing perhaps some disgrace or other dam'age from the Earl's procurement for avoiding thereof, judged it his best course by such wicked means to cause his death by such a long and lingering disease; and two things there were which much encreased this suspition. The one that tho' the Earl had used much endeavour to have the said cook removed, yet could by no means obtain it. The other that the said Cook came to the Earl a little before his death & asked him forgiveness tho' not specifying that thing in Particular. but however it was the good Earl did freely forgive him,

& all others who had any way perhaps concurred thereunto.

He had a great desire to have the assistance of Father Weston at his death by whose means he was first reconciled to the Church: but it would by no means be permitted that either he or any other Priest should come to him. He desired moreover to see his brother ye Lord William Howard, or his Uncle the Ld Henry (made Earl of Northampton afterwards) at least to take his last leave of them before his death; but neither would that be granted, no not so much as to see his brother the Ld Thomas Howard tho' both then and ever he had been a Protestant. The queen had made a kind of promise to some of his friends in his behalf that before his death his wife & children should come unto him. whereupon conceiving that now his time in this world could not be long, he writ humble letters both to her, and some of the Council petitioning the performance of that supposed promise. The Lieutenant of the Tower carryed his letters and delivered them with his own hands to the queen, and brought him this answer from her by word of mouth. That if he would but once go to their church, his request should not only be granted, but he should moreover be restored to his honour, and Estates, with as much favour as she could shew. Which message being delivered he gave thanks to ye Lieutenant for his pains, and said he could not accept her Maties offers upon that condition; adding withall that he was sorry he had but one life to lose for that cause. A very worthy gentleman who was present at this passage has often averr'd it to be true. And I do ye more easily believe it in regard the Lord Buckhurst, afterward Earl of Dorset, who was then of the Queens Council & in great respect, told the same in substance to his son in law the Ld Antony Viscount Mountague, from whose mouth I hear'd it, greatly condemning the good Earl of much want of wisdome and discretion for not accepting so great & gracious a favour, as he esteemed that offer to have been.

Not long after he grew so faint and weak decaying by degrees, that he was not able to rise from his bed. Whereupon by the advice of his Physicians he gave over the saying of his Breviary and the reading of other books, betaking himself only to his beads and some other devotions whereto by vow he had obliged himself; and these he never omitted till the very last day of his life, having his beads almost alwayes with him in his bed. His Physitians comeing to visit him some few dayes before his departure, he desired them not to trouble themselves now any more his case being beyond their skill, and he haveing then some business, meaning his devotions, which he desired, but fear'd he should not have time sufficient to dispatch. And they thereupon departing Sir Michel Blount then Lieutenant of ye Tower who had been ever very hard and harsh unto him, took occasion to come & visit him, & kneeling down by his bedside, in humble manner desired his Lordship to forgive him. Whereto the Earl answered in this manner. Do you ask forgiveness Mr Lieutenant? Why then I forgive you in the same sort as I desire my self to be forgiven at the hands of God. And then kissing his hand offered it in most charitable and kind manner to him, and holding him fast by the hand said. I pray you also to forgive me whatever I have said or done in any thing offensive to you; and he melting into tears and answering that he forgave him with all his heart. The Earl raised himself a little upon his pillow and casting his eyes towards the Lievtenant made a brief and grave speech unto him in this manner. Mr Lievtenant, you have shew'd both me and my men very hard measure. Wherein my Lord quoth he? Nay, said the Earl, I will not make a recapitulation of any thing, for it is all freely forgiven. Only I am to say unto you a few words of my last will, which being observed, may by the grace of God turn much to your benefit and reputation. I speak not for my self, for God of his goodness has taken order that I shall be delivered very short[*l*]y out of your charge: only for others I speak who may be committed to this place. You must think Mr Lievtenant that when a prisoner comes hither to this Tower, that he bringeth sorrow with him. Oh then do not add affliction to affliction: there is no man whatsoever that thinketh himself to stand surest but may fall. It is a very inhuman part to tread on him whom misfortune hath cast down. The man that is void of mercy, God hath in great detestation. Your commission is only to keep with safety, not to kill with severity. Remember good Mr Lievtenant y^t God who with his finger turneth the unstable wheel of this variable world, can in the revolution of a few dayes bring you to be a prisoner also, and to be kept in the same place where now you keep others. There is no calamity that men are subject unto, but you may also taste as well as any other man. Farewell Mr Lieutenant : for the time of my smal abode come to me whenever you please, & you shall be heartily wellcome as my friend. The Lieutenant then humbly took his leave, & went out of the chamber weeping, tho' then perhaps little thinking y^t the Earl's words, or rather prophecy would so soon have been fullfill'd in him: for within seven weeks after the Earl's death, he fell into great disgrace, lost his Office, and was indeed committed and kept close prisoner in the Tower where he had kept others, and another Lieutenant placed, who carry'd as hard a hand over him as he had done over others.

The last night of his life he spent for the most part in prayer, sometimes saying his beads sometimes such psalms and prayers as he knew by heart. And oftentimes used these holy aspirations : O Lord into thy hands I commend my spirit. Lord thou ar't my hope ; and the like. very frequently moreover invocateing the Holy names of Jesus and Mary. Seeing his servants in the morning stand by his bedside weeping in a mournfull manner, he ask'd them what a clock it was ; they answering that it was eight or there about. Why then said he, I have almost run out my course, & come to the end of this miserable and mortal life, desiring them not to weep for him since he did not doubt by the grace of God but all would go well with him. Which being said, he return'd to his prayers upon his beads again, tho' then with a very slow, hollow and fainting voice, & so continued as long as he was able to draw so much breath as was sufficient to sound out the names of Jesus and the glorious Virgin, which were the last words which he was ever heard to speak. The last minute of his last hour being now come, lying on his back, his eies firmly fixt towards heaven, and his long lean consumed armes out of the bed, his hand upon his breast laid in Cross one upon the other, about twelve a clock at noon, in which hour he was also born into this world, arraign'd, condemn'd, and adjudg'd unto death, upon Sunday the 19th of October 1595 (after almost 11 years imprisonment in the tower) in a most sweet manner without any sign of grief or groan, only turning his head a little aside, as one falling into a pleasing sleep, he surrender'd his happy soul into the hands of Almighty God, who to his so great glory had created it.

Some have thought, and perhaps not improbably, that he had some foreknowledg of the day of his death, because about seven or eight dayes before making certain notes (understood only by himself) in his Calendar, what prayers and devotions he intended to say upon every day of the week following, on munday, tuesday, &c. : when he came to the Sunday on which he dy'd, he there made a pause saying, Hitherto and no farther : this is enough : and so writ no more, as his servants who then heared his words, & saw him write, have often testified.

CHAPTER XVIII

His Burial, and other accidents after his Death

His corps remain'd till the tuesday following in the chamber where he dyed, and then being shrouded in a poor sheet, was put into a plain cofin covered with a mean black cloth, and carry'd without any solemnity to the chappell of the Tower, and there buried in the chancel in the very self same grave where the Duke his Father's was: where it did remain till the year 1624 wherein by the procurement of the Countess his wife & the Earl his son it was removed from thence and brought first to her house at West Horseley in Surrey, and being put into an iron coffin, which she caused to be purposely made, and conveniently adorn'd for it, was soon after convey'd to Arundel and there deposited in a vault built at her appointment also, for her self and those of her posterity and family: with this Latin Inscription upon it.

> Philippi Comitis olim Arund. et Sur. ossa veneranda hoc loculo condita, impetratâ a Jacobo Rege veniâ, Annæ Uxoris dilectissimæ cura, Thomæ Filij insigni pietate a Turri Londinensi in hunc locum translata sunt anno 1624. Qui 1mo ob fidei Catho. professionem sub Elizabetha carceri mancipatus, deinde pœnâ pecuniaria 10000 lib. mulctatus, tandem capitis iniquissime condemnatus, post vitam in aretissima custodia in eadem Turri an. 10. mens. 6. sanctissimè transactum piissime, 19 Oct. 1595 non absq' veneni suspitione in Domino obdormivit.

I forgot to note in the due place that upon the night precedent to the Earl's arraignment and condemnation, a nitingale was hear'd to sing with great melody in a Jessamine tree all ye night long in the garden of Arundel house where his Countess and children then did remain, the which may seem the more strange in regard the like was neither before, nor since that time ever heared in that place. Another thing as strange did happen in the Tower soon after his death; for two tame stags which the Lieutenant kept there for his pleasure falling into a fury, never desisted knocking their horns against the walls till their brains being beaten out they dy'd.

I signified before how the Lieu^t. himself within few weeks after the Earl's Death was disgracefully thrust out of his office and put prisoner in the Tower. And now I may add that Sir Thomas Hennage one of his chiefest enimies (the Earl of Leicester and Walsingham being dead before, and both of them most miserably) died in a fearfull manner with great horror & noise within four dayes after his most happy departure. Mr Bennet the Priest one of those who had accused him, fell not long after into a grievous disease whereof he also died miserably with great remorse and grief for what he had done. And Sir Thomas Gerard who was the other, never prospered after that time, but sold and wasted a great part of his Estate, lived a lewd licentious life, fell from the Profession of the Catholick Faith, and so continued till about a year before his death.

CHAPTER XIX

A Description of his Person, & natural gifts

THE Earl was tall of stature, yet ever very streight, long visaged, but of a comely countenance. He was much addicted unto sports and mirth in his youth as being of a pleasant disposition. His memory was excellent, his wit more than ordinary. He was naturally eloquent, & of a ready speech. Whilst he was a Protestant, he once out of merriment disguised himself in the habit of a Minister of the better sort, and going upon a Sunday to the church of a certain Country Town there preached in such manner, that some of good understanding and judgment who were present affirmed they seldom had heared a better sermon nor so well delivered. And this may be an argument of the greatness of his memory, that if he had but once heared out of any English, Latin, or Italian history so much read as was contained in a leaf, he would forthwith perfectly have repeated it. Some for a trial have invented twenty long strange and difficult words, which he had never seen nor heared before, yet did he recite them readily, every one in the same order as they were written, haveing once only read them over. Going one day from the Cathedral Church of St Paul in London to his own house without Temple Bar, he observed the signs of all the houses that were on the left side of the street, which are some hundreds questionless, and being come into his house he caused one of his servants to write them down in a paper as he named them and another being sent with the paper to try thereby if the signs of the houses did agree both in name number, and order with those written in the paper, found them exactly so to do.

Being at the Sessions held at Chichester whilst he was a Protestant, & in Authority in ye Country, he made a very wise and ordered Speech of an hour long concerning some then present affairs of the Kingdome in the presence of the Earl of Northumberland the Lord Viscount Montague, and many Principal

Knights & Gentlemen of the Shire. The day following he took his Journey towards London, and neither in his journey, not for the space of ten dayes after did he make any mention of that Speech, nor indeed scarce had time so much as to think of it, being hindered by many other businesses then occurring, and at the end of those ten dayes he called his Secretary Mr Keeper who was present when he pronounced it (from whose relation I came to have notice of it) and com'anding him to write, he dictated the chief and greatest part of the said Speech in the same words and sentences, as he had recited it at Chichester, never haveing before that hour written one word thereof, but only as he first conceived it in his mind, had till then conserved it in his memory.

Much might be said of the acuteness of his wit shewed by the ready answers which in occasions upon the suddain he would make. But I will content my self with one which he made to a forward Protestant at his being in the Tower, as it was related by the above-named Mr Keeper who well might be, and as I take it, was an ear witness thereof. That Protestant standing by the Earl whilst in time of his recreation he was engraving with his knife ye sign of the Holy Cross in a stone of the wall of his Chamber, and seeing him to have hurt his hand a little by the accidental sliping of the knife, said thus: Your Lordship by this may see, how soon the Lord doth hinder this unlawfull work you were in hand withall. Nay rather, answer'd the Earl, you may mark how quickly the devil hath apply'd himself to frustrate so good an action. The Protestant haveing nothing to reply, the Earl went on with his pious work, and entered into other good discourse. And the same, occasion being offered to speak of Noblemen, he said they were called in Latin *Optimates ab Optimo*, to put them in mind, that in their lives and conversation they should as well endeavour to be the *best*, as they are in place and rank the chief and principal persons in the Commonwealth. Mention moreover being made of worldly goods, he said they were in his conceit like unto dust, as being carry'd with every wind of fortune, now this, now that way from one man to another, or rather like unto shadows, which do not long remain in one settled place and form, nor can be conserved from fading, and soon vanishing away.

CHAPTER XX

Some of his Moral Vertues

THE natural gifts of wit and memory mentioned in the precedent Chapter, though they were extraordinary; yet neither so commendable, not to be compared to the many vertues wherewith he was endow'd. And first: He was so addicted to almesdeeds and compassion of the poor, even before his being Catholick that he not only gave charge always when he went abroad to some one or other of his servants to give unto all those who did demand almes of him, but himself also would sometimes bestow it on some who did not ask it, whereby it often came to pass that when knowledge beforehand was had of his going forth, his coach could scarce pass through the street for the multitude of poor people assembled to receive his charity. Out of this his pious disposition and commiseration of those who were in misery, it proceeded that he could not dissemble any Injury done to them, but would reprehend or admonish thereof those he could conveniently when he saw them at any time to have offended therein, as he did to a certain gentleman at Chichester in this manner. Verily you have too much forgot your self, Good Sir, in abusing such a poor man in the manner you have done it. Far better had it been you had considered that before god there is no difference betwixt the poor and rich, betwixt the beggar and the Gentleman, all of us are of the same nature made of the same mold, enjoying the same air. Those therefore who are of better birth, or higher in degree ought not to contemn others, much less insult over 'em, but rather help and pleasure them.

His gratitude likewise towards all who had ever done him any kind office, good deed, or courtesie was very remarkable. For even to his own servants tho' of the meaner sort, he would not only by wordes thankfully acknowledg any such good turn, but ever bear it in his mind till one way or other he had requited it. And not long before his death he left order how all of them who had done him any service should be abundantly rewarded; some with present money, some with leases, some with annuities, and very sufficient provision during their lives. — I have seen diverse of his letters to the Ld Chancellor, Treasurer and others who sometimes did good offices for him to the queen in the time of his troubles, in which he ever shewed as much thankfullness as might be expressed, & not only to them, but in other letters to his Lady & other private friends, he still did ye same whensoever there was any occasion to mention the Courtesies which Noble men had done him.

But yet none so much, as those from whom he had received any comfort, counsel, or direction tending to the good of his soul; as among others to F^r Robert Southwell, the which he expressed in this manner in one amongst diverse other letters written to that effect. My Dear and R^d Father. This being the last time that I think I shall ever send unto you, I should be very ungratefull if, wanting all other means of expressing my thankfullness I shou'd not now at least acknowledg it in words; and as I must needs say, I could not be more bound to any man, nor to any but one of your calling so much; and all this in a time when such comforts were most wellcome, and even to the benefit of that which in all men is most pretious: so in heart, our Lord who sees all secrets, sees my good will and thankfullness, and I doubt not will reward you amongst all your other worthy merits, for these bestowed on me his most unworthy servant; and in as much thankfullness and good will as my heart can conceive, I remain yours till the last moment. And that this was not out of complement, but real and unfeined, appeared by the love and respect he always did bear him: for when the said Father after some years was apprehended and imprisoned in the Tower, whensoever the Lieu$^{t\cdot}$ made any mention of him in his presence, as oftentimes he did, he used ever to speak with great respect of him, calling him often, *Blessed Father.* and when once the Lieutenant seemed to take exceptions thereat saying: Term you him Blessed Father being as he is an enimy to his Country? The Earl defended him, saying: How can that be, seeing your self hath told me heretofore that no fault could be laid unto him, but his Religion. And the Lieu^t telling him at another time, that his (the Earl's) dog came into Father Southwell's chamber whilst he was there with him, he answered that he loved his dog the better for it, and the Lieutenant in a scoffing manner saying it might be the dog came thither to have his blessing; the Earl reply'd, it was no news for irrational creatures to seek blessing at the hands of holy men, Saint Jerome writing how those Lions which had digged with their paws St Paul the Eremit's grave stood after waiting with their eyes upon St Antony expecting his blessing.

The like gratefull mind and great affection he also ever bore and alwayes shew'd unto F^r William Weston by whom he was first reconciled, and for his sake unto the wholl society; for thus he writ in a letter to one of them. I call God to witness I have, and do principally in my heart most affect, reverence, and honour your vocation above others, for that I have seen, hear'd, and read, as also in respect that from one of that calling I received the greatest good which ever I tasted.

The great humility of his mind appeared also many wayes, as in his apparel which ever after his becomeing Catholick was alwayes very plain. His gowns which I have seen being no better than ordinary broad cloth, the faceing and capes of bayes without any manner of lace or other ornament, and the rest of his apparell was proportionable to his gowns. Secondly in his words and conversation, being very Courteous and affable even to the meanest, and in point of vertue preferring all others before himself. From whence it proceeded that in many occasions he term'd himself The unworthyest of God's servants. Thirdly in his willingness to be advised of his faults, oversights & imperfections: for thus I find him saying in one of his letters to F^r Southwell. What fault soever you shall upon your own knowledg find to be in me, and tell me of, I will always endeavour and desire to amend. And this he really ever performed as I have perceived by diverse of his letters to his Lady and others wherein he gave order for the amending of some things whereof he had been advised by the said Father, whose directions he had resolved so exactly to observe, that in a matter which did no less concern him than his life, he thus writ unto his Lady: Assure him from me, (sayes he speaking of F^r Southwell) that I will not for any worldly respect whatsoever, God willing, go one inch farther than he doth direct. Lastly the like humility he shew'd in the smal conceit he had of his own writings and all other things which he did: for how well soever they were done in the judgment of others, yet did he think them full of imperfections and faults; as those treatises which he compiled in the praise of Vertue, were judged by him to contain great faults and gross errors, in wch respect he willed his Secretary Mr Keeper to deliver them to F^r Weston to be corrected. I pray you, sayes he, if it please God to call me, make this humble petition for me to that Blessed Father to whose will you shall commit that work, that as Charity covereth many faults, so my charitable intent therein to do good to all, and not willingly offend any, may obtain a pardon for all my gross faults, and absurd errors.

CHAPTER XXI

The care of his Conscience, and Sorrow for his Sins

I HAVE already spoken of his Devotion & much application unto Prayer : and therefore will now only add that the very first time he had an opportunity of writing to his Lady after his imprisonment, he sent for the Office of the B^d Virgin and a book treating of the Rosary to the end he might the better understand how to say it for the best benefit of his soul, and ever after such things as were tending to piety were always most wellcome unto him : his only care being about the serving of Almighty God, and the conserving his conscience free from any thing that might trouble it. To that end he gave order to his officers, that not only his own and his Fathers debts should be forthwith pay'd, but that also all wrongs done to any either in his own, his Fathers or Great grandfathers dayes, should be compleatly satisfied.

I might here set down many examples of the tenderness of his conscience, and fear to do any thing that might be offensive unto God ; but I will content my self with these few following. The Duke his Father sent him an English Bible of the Protestants translation not long before his Death ; the which for that reason he kept very carefully till he became Catholick. This bible I know not by what means was brought into the Tower ; wherein because his Keepers and the Lieutenant's men did sometimes read, he was so troubled at it (tho' he knew right well if that had not been there they would have procured some other) that he resolv'd to have written to the Ld Chancellor for a warrant (without which it could not be done) to have it sent away, and infallibly he would have so done, had it not before by accident come into his hands, and so was kept ever safe from doing hurt to any. The Gentleman who was his Keeper told him soon after his condemnation, that he intended, in speaking to some Lords about him, to say, that tho' now expecting to die, he found him very resolute in his Religion, yet he hoped some good might be done with him if there were any assurance of his life. Not doubting, as he said, but such kind of speeches, tho' utter'd only as his own opinion might be a means for the saving of his (the Earl's) life. To which he answered in this manner. You know I never gave you the least hope of any such thing : and I would have you know most assuredly, that tho' I live I will never alter one jot of my faith. yet as for saying so out of your own opinion, I leave it to your self, if you think it may do me any good. Of these last words he was very fearfull afterwardes lest they might be some way scandalous, and therefore writ to his Lady to consult with some men of Learning about them, assureing her if they should be so thought he would expressly forbid his Keeper to speak in that manner. In his Examinations, and at his trial at Westminster before the Lords his Peers he ever constantly denied that he either willed Mr Bennet the Priest to say a Mass of the Holy Ghost for ye success of the Spanish fleet, or that he told either Sir Thomas Gerard or Mr Shelley that the prayer of 24 hours should be for that intention, and in his private letters to his Lady, he often did the same, adding withall, as she told me, that he was so newly made a Catholick before his imprisonment, that he knew not that there was any such Mass as of the Holy Ghost. Yet after his condemnation writing to Father Southwell (tho' therein he doth protest he could not remember that ever he had said any such thing to Mr Shelly, or that he ever mention'd a Mass of the Holy Ghost to Mr Bennet) he desired to know whether it were any burden or no in conscience unto him to have so resolutely denied those things, seing on the one side they upon their oaths had testified that he did them, and on the other he knew really he had wished well to the Spaniards in his Speeches, tho' he could not call to mind he had done that of which he was by them accused. And of this he desired to be resolved, as he said, out of a fear of doing wrong to his accusers, being ready at his execution, which he then expected every day, to charge himself with the most, lest they might be thought by many to have altogether untruly accused him. Entreating Father Southwell moreover to signifie as much unto his wife and other friends, lest they might remain wth the same evill opinion of his accusers, in case he judged him in conscience bound thereto, now that he had truely manifested unto him as much as possibly he could say in their behalf against himself.

Now how great his sorrow and repentance was for his sins committed against Alm. God, may be conjectured by what he manifested in diverse of his letters to have had of the neglect, and ill usage of his Lady in his younger years, whilst he was a Protestant. In one to her self thus he writ. Mine own good wife. I must now in this world take my last farewell of you, and as I know no person living whom I have so much offended as your self, so do I account this opportunity of asking you forgiveness, as a singular benefit of almighty God, and I most humbly and hartily beseech you even for his sake, and of your charity to forgive me all whereinsoever I have offended you, and the assurance thereof is a great contentment to my soul at this present, and will be a greater I doubt not when it is ready to depart out of my body, and I call God to witness it is no smal grief unto me that I can'ot make you recompence in this world for the wrongs I have done you; for if it had pleased God to have granted me longer life, I doubt not but you should have found me as good a husband to my poor ability by his grace, as you have found me bad heretofore. In one to F^r Southwell speaking covertly of her he sayes, I call our Lord to witness that as no sin grieves me any thing so much as my offences to that party (his Lady) so no worldly thing makes me loather to depart hence than that I cannot live to make that party satisfaction according to my most ardent and affectionate desire. *Afflictio dat intellectum*, affliction gives understanding. God I hope of his infinit mercy who knows my heart, & has seen my true sorrow in that behalf has remitted all I doubt not, and so has the party of her singular charity to my unspeakable comfort. To another friend thus: I pray you tell my wife, that if I live, next to the comfort that I shall reap thereby of having opportunity to make satisfaction by pennance for my heinous and manifold sins against Alm. God; my greatest joy is that thereby I shall shew her what a great desire I have, (if I had been able) to have made amends in some part for the many and great injuries which I have done her. Finally in another to her self: he that knows all things, knows that which is past is a nail in my conscience, and burden the greatest I feel there : my will is to make satisfaction, if my ability were able : but tho' I should live never so long, I could never do it further than by a good desire to do it, which while I have any spark of breath shall never be wanting.

CHAPTER XXII

His constancy in the Catholick Faith

Altho' his constancy in the Catholick Religion was manifest to the world, and hath been already sufficiently declared, yet it will not be amiss out of his own letters here to insert some clauses whereby the same may more clearly appear. And first, thus he writ in one to F^r Southwell soon after his condemnation. It is my dayly prayer I call our Lord to witness, that I may continue constant in the profession of his Catholick faith to the end, and in the end, come life or death or whatsoever els. And he knows, who knows the secrets of all hearts, that I am fully resolved to endure any death, rather than willingly yield to any thing offensive to his divine Majesty in the least respect, or to give just cause of scandal to the meanest Catholick. And in another not long after to the same Father. Assure your self I will never to save my life accuse my self unjustly or belie myself and so have told my Keeper more than once, and God who knows the secrets of all hearts, knows that I am ready to endure any death than deny, or stagger in the least point of my Faith.

The like he signified in many other Letters written about that time both to the same Father and to his Lady. And in one to Mr Keeper some years after, and not long before his own and F^r Southwell's death who then was in the Tower thus he saith. For which Religion my self have allready laid down my life, and am at all times ready to leave it whensoever in that quarrell it shall be demanded if all the lives of the men in the world were included in my neck, and this God knows to be true.

About a year or a little more after his committment to the Tower, one Mr MacWilliams who had the Keeping of him for a time, at his departure told him that if he would but shew so much conformity as to read books, both he and others thought it would draw him out of the Tower; whereupon giving notice of it to his Lady he writ in these words: I know it is not unlawfull, if a man have leave, and I am sure by the grace of God that none of their false books shall make me as much as once to stagger in my faith. Wherefore I pray let some zealous, learned & discreet man be talked withall, and sue for leave for me at his hands if he shall think it lawfull, and that I may do it without any scandal in the world to the Church; otherwise I would rather choose to lie here all the dayes of my life, than by any act for my liberty offend or scandalize the smalest member of the Catholick Church.

Another of his Keepers after his condemnation told him first that the Ld Treasurer did much desire he would admit some minister to come unto him and hear what he could say about religion. But he in no case would yield thereunto, tho' otherwise he were very desirous to gratify that Nobleman whom he ever esteemed as a special friend, because he thought the doing thereof would argue in him a wavering or doubtfullness which in matter of Religion, as he said, is as much as a deniall of it. Afterwards he signify'd unto him, if he would at least seem to desire that a Priest and Minister might be brought jointly both before him to hear them two dispute together, that ye queen would receive much satisfaction therewith, & perhaps be moved to do much good unto him. He answer'd that he would not have any such motion made as proceeding from him lest it might seem to argue some doubt of his faith; and that he would never so admit of any such thing as the queen or any other might have any cause of hope, that he would ever alter his religion wherein by the grace of God he was most resolute. And lastly, if he ever did admitt thereof it should be first upon the queen's express command, and next with this protestation that he did it only to satisfie her, thinking the thing to be lawfull, and not doubting, but being most resolute in every point & tittle of his Faith. And he thought it lawfull in regard, as he signify'd to F^r Southwell, he remember'd that F^r Weston had once told him he might admitt of a Minister offered or urged upon him, so that he had a Priest allow'd who could answer and detect his untruths. Adding withall that peradventure such a disputation might by the grace of God work some unexpected good towards some who were most forward to procure it, if they were not too far given over.

CHAPTER XXIII

His chearfullness in suffering, & confidence in God

MUCH might be said of his willingness and contentment in suffering and endureing such crosses and afflictions as befell him during his long imprisonment: but I will satisfy my self with only setting down his own words taken out of some of his letters, which I have seen. First therefore in one to F^r Southwell thus he sayes. For all Crosses touching worldly matters, I thank God they trouble me not much, and much the less for your singular good Counsel, which I beseech our Lord I may often remember. In another about some vile slanders raised of him which I have already mentioned in the Eleventh Chapter, these be his words. I assure you I thank our Lord these slanders trouble me no whit, but rather yield me comfort considering that I sustain them for his name.

In one to his Lady a little before his last troubles he writes thus. I beseech you for the love of God to comfort your self whatsoever shall happen, and to be best pleased with that, which shall please God best and be his will to send. For mine own part I find by more arguments than those I understand from you that there is some intent (as they think who work it) to do me no good, but indeed to do me the most good of all. but I am I thank God, and doubt not but I shall be by his grace ready to endure the worst which flesh and blood can do against me. And so indeed he declared himself really to be by the courage, chearfullness and alacrity which he shewed at the time of his arraignment, and in all occasions when his adversaries were most violent against him. For, such and so great it was, that the Gentleman who then was his Keeper, told him many thereby judg'd him as desperate, and some of his friends wondered he would speak so roundly to those who were his examiners in the Tower about the business whereof he was afterwards arraigned, telling one of them, as I said before, that he cared not for the worst he could do against him : and to another, who threatened him with hanging, That the sooner the better if it pleas'd God it should be so. The which he did, as he signified to F^r Southwell, to shew that he regarded not their threats : not out of any anger, sayes he, or malice towards them, but to let them know my conscience being clear, & my cause good, that I cared not for the worst they could do against me.

That which chiefly caused this courage & chearfullness in him, was the great confidence he had in the mercy and goodness of Almighty God, that he would ever help and assist him in all occasions : for so he writ to a friend whom he certified of his readiness and chearfullness to enter into the last combat at that time when he look'd every day to be carry'd to execution. I assure you I prepare my self as much as my weakness and frailty will permitt, and I had rather perform more, than come short of that I promise, especially wherein my frailty and unworthiness and infinit sins may justly make me doubt of the performance. But I know God's mercy is above all and I am sure he will never suffer me to be tempted above my strength; and upon this I build with all assurance and comfort. And in another to his Lady : I beseech you, take all as well as you may, assuring your self God doth all for the best to those y^t love him, and suffers none to be tempted above their strength, and upon these two I have cast my anchor of hope.

CHAPTER XXIV

His Charity & Good Desires

How great his Charity was towards God and his neighbor may appear as well by his desire of doing and suffering for God's sake, as by his willingness to pardon and forgive all injuries received from any man. In a letter to a friend of his wherein he complain'd that Sir Thomas Gerard had done both most uncharitably & unjustly in accusing him of diverse things, he therein did protest, that freely and from his heart he did forgive him all. The like he did to Mr Bennet and all those who had wrongfully given Testimony against him. As also to those who had raised most vile slanders against him, as that he was of no Religion and the like.

Not long before his death when he was so weak and feeble that he was scarce able without help to walk from one end of his chamber to the other, pointing with his finger towards the Tower hill, he told his servants who then supported him; that had it been Gods will, he desired much more to have died for his faith upon that hill, than in his bed and chamber, as now it seemed likely he should do : and that tho' he had often consulted the Phisicians in the time of his sickness, it was not so much out of any great desire of living long, as some perhaps might think, as to conserve himself untill he should see if it were Gods holy pleasure that he should die publickly for his Religion. To the which he prepar'd himself a long time with great diligence by fasting, prayer, meditation, and diverse other pious exercises wherein yet he far less confided (such was his vertue and humility) than in the prayers and good endeavors of others for him. In which respect he both oft and earnestly beg'd them, and in particular in one Letter to F^r Southwell after this manner. I beseech you for the love of God, procure me to be remember'd in the morning of my execution in as many ways as you can by that meane which you know most effectual to do me good, and by one of them (that is a

Mass) at the hour of my last conflict as near as may be conjectured.

Concerning his good desires and purposes, if God had given him life to see better times, than those in which he lived, tho' I doubt not they were many more than I have had notice of, yet these three following I find expressed in some letters which he writ to his Lady from the Tower. First that he meant to have made two of his principal houses religious places, and restored all the religious lands in his possession; for thus he said. I pray you let my Son know when he comes to any years of discretion, that I was fully resolved to make Howard-house and Norwich-house religious houses, and to restore all religious lands (if I had lived to see a Catholick time) and desire him for the love of God and on my blessing to do the like (for so God will prosper him) except he shall be otherwise advised by such as I submitt my self to their judgment. Secondly he intended of new to have founded a Chantry, whereof he writ in these words. I have appointed 2500$^{ll.}$ for the building of a Chantry, which I wish my Son to do, if ever he be able, or those that have dealing in my lands before he come of age, if the time serve, and the lands be restored. lastly he was resolved in case he outlived his Lady to have left the world, and become Religious, for thus he sayes. I call God to witness that if it were not in respect of you (albeit I lived) every body should well see, if I were not utterly kept from it against my will, that I esteem as little of the world, as she by her usage has seemed to esteem of me, and that I despised her as much as she did me. And a little after. If you should not do well, I would, if the queen took me not away by a violent death, voluntarily sequester my self from this sea of misery, or els want of my will.

CHAPTER XXV

The great good Estimation others had of Him

THE Vertues of the Earl whereof hitherto I have spoken together with many more not mentioned by me, were so excellent, and shined in such manner, that not only the Catholicks of this kingdome and nation; but of many others were much edified thereby, and for them did highly esteem, love and honour him. And so great was the respect and affection which all generally here in England did bear him that one of good rank amongst them told one of those gentlemen who had the custody of him, y^t he had wonne all the Catholicks hearts of ye Kingdome by the good usage he had shewn to the Earl his prisoner. And in other nations some of great learning, and some both of learning and dignity have left large Encomiums written in his praise, as the most Reverend Diego de Yepes Bishop of Taracona in Spain, and some others in France and Italy which I will not now stand to relate, contenting my self with that which I find written by the Reverend Father Cornelius a Lapide of the Flemish nation a Learned Religious of the Society of Jesus in his commentaries upon the 10th Chapter of the Epistle to the Hebrews, upon those words of the 34 verse. *Rapinam bonorum vestrorum en gaudio suscepistis.* where he speaks of him in this manner.

The most Noble Earl of Arundel Philipp Howard son and heir of the Duke of Norfolk, being taken when he was flying into France for the Catholick Religion, was cast into the Tower of London, and afterwards arraigned and condemned and after ten years and a half imprisonment or there about, he died in durance a Glorious Confessor, yea a Martyr. He was the chief Earl of England, and of a Most Noble Family: and wonderfull it is how much he lost, and with what quietness of mind he endured all adversities. Whilst he was prisoner he was not only of Example, but a singular comfort to all Catholicks. No one ever hear'd him complain either of the loss of his goods, or of the incommodities of the prison, or the being bereaved of his liberty : and such as he heared complaine or understood to be aggrieved, he endeavoured by his words and courteous usage to comfort, strengthen, and confirm. His delight was in nothing but in God, and the contemplation of heavenly things. Much of the money which the Queen did allow him for his maintenance (for to every prisoner in the Tower something is assigned, more or less according to each man's degree) he gave unto the poor, contenting himself with a spare and slender diet. Many other things this Most Noble Earl said, did, and suffered, which equalise, if not exceed the deeds of the ancient worthies of the Primitive Church and therefore are most worthy to be eternized.

That which this Author saith of the Earl that he was a Glorious Confessor of the Catholick Faith, yea a Martyr, is the General perswasion of all Learned Catholick men, both of our own and other nations. As such therefore we all ought to esteem him, and may with just reason commend our selves to his Holy prayers and Intercession, that thereby we may obtain so much grace of Almighty God, that here we may imitate his excellent Vertues, and in heaven enjoy his happy company for all Eternity.   Amen.

BIOGRAPHICAL NOTES ON PERSONS MENTIONED IN THE NARRATIVE

ALBRIDGE, MRS. Presumably Jane, widow of Solomon Aldred, who became the second wife of Dr. Thomas Lodge, q.v.

ALLEN, WILLIAM (1532–1594), of Rossall, co. Lancs. Created Cardinal, 7 Aug. 1587.

ARUNDEL, ANNE, COUNTESS OF (1557–1630), dau. of Thomas, Lord Dacre of Gilsland by Elizabeth Leyburne who became the 3rd wife of Thomas, 4th Duke of Norfolk. She married ST. PHILIP HOWARD in 1571 and is buried at Arundel. Previously styled Countess of Surrey.

ARUNDEL, HENRY FITZALAN, EARL OF (1512–1579/80). His first wife was Catharine, dau. of Thomas Grey, 2nd Marquess of Dorset and the mother of Lady Mary Fitzalan who married, as his first wife, Thomas Howard, 4th Duke of Norfolk.

AUDLEY, MARGARET (1540–1563/4), dau. of Thomas Audley, Baron Audley of Walden. She was the widow of Lord Henry Dudley and married Thomas Howard, 4th Duke of Norfolk, as his second wife, between 10 Dec. 1558 and 2 March 1558/9.

AUDLEY, SIR THOMAS (1488–1544). Lord Chancellor, 1533; created Baron Audley of Walden, 1538; founder of Magdalene College, Cambridge.

BALE, JOHN (1495–1563), Bishop of Ossory.

BENNET, WILLIAM. Priest; for his confession, 16 Oct. 1588, see Catholic Record Society, vol. 21 (1919), pp. 185-187.

BLOUNT, SIR MICHAEL, Lieutenant of the Tower of London.

BRAY, WILLIAM, servant of ST. PHILIP HOWARD.

BRIDGES *alias* GRATELY, EDWARD, a priest.

BROMLEY, SIR THOMAS (1530–1587), Lord Chancellor from 1579 to 1587; presided over the trial of Mary, Queen of Scots in 1586.

BUCKHURST. See Dorset, Earls of.

BURLACE OR BURLACY, CHRISTOPHER, servant of ST. PHILIP HOWARD.

CAMPION, EDMUND (1539/40–1581), of London. Executed at Tyburn, and one of the forty martyrs of England and Wales.

CAREY, SIR GEORGE (*c.* 1555–1603), son of Henry Carey, 1st Lord Hunsdon, q.v. Knighted for his military services at Berwick, 11 May, 1570; appointed Marshal of the Queen's Household, 18 March 1580/1; Lord Chamberlain of the Household, 1597–1603; succeeded his father as 2nd Baron Hunsdon, 1596.

CECIL, SIR WILLIAM (1520–1598), statesman; created Baron of Burghley, Lord High Treasurer from 1572 and chief minister of Queen Elizabeth I.

CHARKE, WILLIAM (*fl.* 1580), Puritan; Fellow of Peterhouse, Cambridge; preacher to Lincoln's Inn, 1581–1593.

DACRE, ANNE (1557–1630). See Arundel, Anne, Countess of.

DACRE (of Gilsland), ELIZABETH, LADY (d. 1567), dau. of Sir James Leyburne, of Cunswick, co. Westmorland, 2nd wife of Thomas, Lord Dacre of Gilsland and 3rd wife of Thomas, 4th Duke of Norfolk.

DACRE, ELIZABETH. See Howard, Lady Elizabeth.

DACRE (of Gilsland), GEORGE DACRE, LORD (*c.* 1562–1569), son of Thomas, Lord

Dacre and Elizabeth (née Leyburne). He d. 17 May 1569, from a fall off a wooden horse, at Thetford, co. Norfolk.

DACRE (of Gilsland), THOMAS DACRE, LORD (*c.* 1525–1566). His 2nd wife was Elizabeth, dau. of Sir James Leyburne; she married Thomas, 4th Duke of Norfolk, as his 3rd wife.

DIX or DYX, WILLIAM, steward of the Norfolk estates of the Duke of Norfolk. In a copy of the New Testament now at Arundel Castle is a farewell letter to "good Dyx" written on 10 February 1571/2 by Thomas, 4th Duke of Norfolk, who was daily expecting to be executed. The Duke asks Dyx to 'Forgett not w^t plannes to cowncell and advyse Phylyps and Nannes unexperycncyd yeares . . .'.

DORSET, MARGARET, COUNTESS OF (d. 1591), dau. and heir of Thomas, 4th Duke of Norfolk. She was the 1st wife of Robert Sackville, 2nd Earl of Dorset.

DORSET, ROBERT SACKVILLE, EARL OF (1561–1608/9), son of Thomas Sackville, Baron of Buckhurst and Earl of Dorset. He married, as his 1st wife, Margaret, dau. and heir of Thomas, 4th Duke of Norfolk; she died 19 Aug. 1591.

DORSET, THOMAS SACKVILLE, EARL OF (born between 1527 and 1536; d. 1608). Knighted by Thomas, 4th Duke of Norfolk, 8 June 1567, in the presence of the Queen at Westminster, and created Baron of Buckhurst, co. Sussex. Created Earl of Dorset in 1603/4.

DUN, HENRY, servant of Sir Christopher Hatton.

ELIZABETH I, QUEEN (1533–1602/3),dau. of Henry VIII and Anne Boleyn; succeeded Mary I in 1558.

FITZALAN, LADY MARY (1540–1557), dau. of Henry Fitzalan, Earl of Arundel. She was the 1st wife of Thomas Howard, 4th Duke of Norfolk and mother of ST. PHILIP HOWARD.

FOXE, JOHN (1516–1587), martyrologist. His *Actes and Monuments,* popularly known as *The Book of Martyrs,* first printed in English in 1563. Attended his former pupil, Thomas, 4th Duke of Norfolk, at his execution in 1572.

FULKE, WILLIAM (1538–1589), Puritan divine; Master of Pembroke College, Cambridge, from 1578.

GERARD, SIR THOMAS (d. 1601). Of Kingsley, co. Chester, and Bryn, co. Lancs.; M.P. for Lancashire, 1566–7, and High Sheriff of that county, 1558. Accused of a design to deliver Mary, Queen of Scots, was committed to the Tower. For his confession, 25 Oct. 1588, see Catholic Record Society vol. 21 (1919), pp. 187-190.

GIFFORD or GIFFARD, GILBERT (1561?–1590), Roman Catholic spy; died in prison at Paris.

GRANADA, LUIS DE (1505–1588), an eloquent preacher and author of numerous devotional works.

GRATELY *alias* BRIDGES, EDWARD , a priest.

HATTON, SIR CHRISTOPHER (1540–1591), Lord Chancellor from 1587; had been appointed Captain of the Queen's Bodyguard in 1572.

HEATH, NICHOLAS (1501?–1578), the last Catholic Archbishop of York.

HENEAGE, SIR THOMAS (d. 1595), Vice-Chamberlain to Queen Elizabeth I and Privy Councillor from 1589.

HENRY VIII, KING (1491–1546/7), son of Henry VII and Elizabeth Plantagenet, ledest dau. of Edward IV; succeeded Henry VII in 1509.

HEYDON, SIR CHRISTOPHER (d. 1623), writer on astrology; M.P. for Norfolk, 1588; knighted at the capture of Cadiz, 1596; suspected of complicity in the Essex rising, 1601.

HOWARD, LADY ELIZABETH, dau. of Thomas, Lord Dacre of Gilsland (by Elizabeth Leyburne who became the 3rd wife of Thomas, 4th Duke of Norfolk). Married Lord William Howard (brother of ST. PHILIP HOWARD) in 1577.

HOWARD, LORD HENRY. See Northampton, Henry Howard, Earl of.

HOWARD, LORD THOMAS (1561–1626), son of Thomas, 4th Duke of Norfolk by his 2nd wife, Margaret Audley; step-brother of ST. PHILIP HOWARD. Lord Thomas was summoned to Parliament as Baron Howard de Walden in 1597 and created Earl of Suffolk in 1603. His 1st wife was Mary, dau. of Thomas, Lord Dacre of Gilsland.

HOWARD, LORD WILLIAM (1563–1640), son of Thomas, 4th Duke of Norfolk by his 2nd wife, Margaret Audley; step-brother of ST. PHILIP HOWARD. Known as Lord William Howard of Naworth, co. Cumberland; married Elizabeth, dau. of Thomas, Lord Dacre of Gilsland in 1577.

HOWARD. See also under Arundel, Fitzalan, Norfolk, Richmond and Surrey.

HUNSDON, HENRY CAREY, BARON (1525/6–1596). Created a Baron, 13 Jan. 1558/9; Keeper of Somerset House where he died.

HUNTINGDON, HENRY HASTINGS, EARL OF (c. 1536–1595). Lord President of the North from 1572 until his death; was on the trial of Thomas, 4th Duke of Norfolk.

JAMES I, KING (1566–1625). Son of Mary, Queen of Scots and Henry, Lord Darnley (Duke of Albany, Earl of Ross, and Lord Ardmanach); succeeded his mother as James VI of Scotland in 1567 and succeeded Queen Elizabeth I as James I of England in 1602/3.

KEEPER, JOHN. Secretary to SIR PHILIP HOWARD

KELOWAY, CAPTAIN — .

KNOLLYS, SIR FRANCIS (1514?–1596), statesman; Privy Councillor, 1558; M.P. for Arundel, 1559; Treasurer of the Royal Household from 1572.

LABOURN. See Leyburne.

LANSPERGIUS. More generally known, perhaps, as Johann Justus, *Landsberger*. The translation referred to in the text was printed in Antwerp in 1595; there was another edition in 1867.

LAPIDE, CORNELIUS A (d. 1637), a learned and pious Jesuit who wrote commentaries on all the books of the Bible. Died in Rome.

LEICESTER, ROBERT DUDLEY, EARL OF (1532 or 1533–1588). He took part (with his father, John Dudley, Duke of Northumberland) in proclaiming Lady Jane Grey as Queen; was eventually restored in blood; K. G. and Privy Councillor. His first wife was Amy, dau. of Sir John Robsart and she was found dead in Cumnor Place, co. Berks., 8 Sept. 1560. Leicester entertained Queen Elizabeth I at Kenilworth, co. Warw., from 9 to 27 July 1575 at a cost of about £60,000.

LEYBURNE, SIR JAMES, of Cunswick, co. Westmorland. His dau. Elizabeth was the 2nd wife of Thomas, Lord Dacre of Gilsland and 3rd wife of Thomas, 4th Duke of Norfolk.

LODGE, THOMAS (1558?–1625), author, poet and physician. His 2nd wife was Jane, widow of Solomon Aldred, at one time agent to Walsingham at Rome.

LORD CHANCELLOR. See Audley, Sir Thomas; Bromley, Sir Thomas; Hatton, Sir Christopher. For a complete list of Lord Chancellors, etc. of England, see J. Haydn and H. Ockerby, *The Book of Dignities* (1894), pp. 352–358.

LUMLEY, JANE, LADY (d. 1576), elder dau. and coheiress of Henry Fitzalan, Earl of Arundel by his 1st wife, Catharine, dau. of Thomas Grey, Marquess of Dorset. She married John Lumley (afterwards Baron Lumley) who died in 1609.

MACWILLIAMS, MR. Attendant on ST. PHILIP HOWARD while in the Tower; probably a member of the Mackwilliam family of Stambourne, co. Essex.

MARTIN, GREGORY (d. 1582), biblical translator, priest, and tutor to the sons of Thomas, 4th Duke of Norfolk.

MARY I, QUEEN (1515/16–1558), dau. of Henry VIII and Katherine of Arragon; succeeded Edward VI in 1553 and married Philip II, King of Spain in 1554.

MARY, QUEEN OF SCOTS (1542–1586/7), dau. of James V of Scotland and Marie de Lorraine. Mary, Queen of Scots was executed in Fotheringhay Castle, co. Northants., 8 Feb. 1586/7, and there are several relics of her at Arundel Castle.

MOMFORD, JOHN. Secretary to ST. PHILIP HOWARD.

MONTAGU, ANTHONY BROWNE, 1ST VISCOUNT (c. 1528–1592). One of the Commissioners for the trial of Mary, Queen of Scots, 1586. His 2nd wife was Magdalen, dau. of William, 3rd Lord Dacre of Gilsland.

MONTAGU, ANTHONY MARIA BROWNE, 2ND VISCOUNT (1573/4–1629). Married Jane, dau. of Thomas Sackville, Earl of Dorset.

NORFOLK, ELIZABETH, DUCHESS OF (1497?–1558), dau. of Edward Stafford, Duke of Buckingham. She was the 2nd wife of Thomas Howard, 3rd Duke of Norfolk, and Godmother to ST. PHILIP HOWARD.

NORFOLK, MARGARET, DUCHESS OF. See Audley, Margaret.

NORFOLK, MARY, DUCHESS OF. See Fitzalan, Mary.

NORFOLK, THOMAS HOWARD, 3RD DUKE OF (1473–1554). Son of Thomas Howard, 2nd Duke of Norfolk by his 1st wife, Elizabeth, dau. and heir of Sir Frederick Tylney and widow of Sir Humphrey Bourchier. The 3rd Duke of Norfolk was great-grandfather of ST. PHILIP HOWARD.

NORFOLK, THOMAS HOWARD, 4TH DUKE OF (1537/8–1572). Son of Henry Howard, Earl of Surrey, the poet. He married: 1st, Mary, dau. of Henry Fitzalan, Earl of Arundel and she was the mother of ST. PHILIP HOWARD; she died in 1557; 2nd, Margaret, dau. of Thomas Audley, Baron Audley of Walden and she died in 1563/4; 3rd, Elizabeth, dau. of Sir James Leyburne of Cunswick, co. Westmorland, widow of Thomas, Lord Dacre of Gilsland, and she died in 1567. The 4th Duke of Norfolk was beheaded on Tower Hill on 2 June 1572.

NORTHAMPTON, HENRY HOWARD, EARL OF (1539/40–1614). Younger brother of Thomas, 4th Duke of Norfolk; created Baron of Marnhull and Earl of Northampton, 13 March 1603/4.

NORTHUMBERLAND, HENRY PERCY, 2ND EARL OF (c. 1532–1585), brother of Thomas 1st Earl of Northumberland.

NORTHUMBERLAND, THOMAS PERCY, 1ST EARL OF (1528–1572).

NORTON, —, rack master.

PHILIP II, KING OF SPAIN, son of the Emperor Charles V; married Queen Mary I in 1554.

PIGEON, —. Not identified.

POPE SIXTUS V. Succeeded Gregory XIII in 1585 and died in 1590.

RAINBERDE, NICHOLAS. A former servant of ST. PHILIP HOWARD.

RICHMOND, MARY, DUCHESS OF (d. 1557), dau. of Thomas, 3rd Duke of Norfolk, by his 2nd wife, Elizabeth, dau. of Edward Stafford, Duke of Buckingham. Mary married, in 1533, Henry Fitzroy (illegitimate son of Henry VIII by Elizabeth Blount) who had been created Earl of Nottingham and Duke of Richmond and Somerset in 1525.

ROGER, —. An officer in the Tower of London.

SACKVILLE. See Dorset.

SHELLEY, WILLIAM (d. 1597). Of Michelgrove in Clapham, co. Sussex and Southampton. His 1st wife was Margaret, dau. of Thomas Wriothesley, Earl of Southampton. At Shelley's trial for treason, Feb. 1585/6, John, Lord Lumley, was one of the Commissioners.

SHERWIN, RALPH (1550–1581), executed at Tyburn with Edmund Campion. Sherwin is another of the forty martyrs of England and Wales.

SOUTHAMPTON, THOMAS WRIOTHESLEY, EARL OF (1505–1550). A Commissioner for the trial of Henry, Earl of Surrey, 1546/7.

SOUTHWELL, ROBERT (1561?–1595), of Horsham St. Faith, co. Norfolk. Jesuit and poet who was executed at Tyburn, and is another of the forty martyrs of England and Wales.

SURREY, ANNE, COUNTESS OF. See Arundel, Anne, Countess of.

SURREY, HENRY HOWARD, EARL OF (1517?–1546/7), poet. Son of Thomas, 3rd Duke of Norfolk by his 2nd wife, Elizabeth, dau. of Edward Stafford, Duke of Buckingham. The Earl, grandfather of ST. PHILIP HOWARD, was executed on Tower Hill, 19 Jan. 1546/7.

WALGRAVE, NICHOLAS. Servant to ST. PHILIP HOWARD. The name is sometimes written as Wangrave, Wetgrave or Wilgrave.

WALSINGHAM, SIR FRANCIS (1530?–1590), statesman and a zealous Protestant. Secretary of State from 1573.

WESTON, WILLIAM (1550?–1615), Superior of the Jesuit mission in Englnad, 1584; known also as Edmonds and Hunt. Suffered various terms of imprisonment; died at Valladolid.

WHITAKERS. Probably William Whitaker (1548–1595), Master of St. John's College, Cambridge, from 1586; interpreted the teaching of the Church of England in its most Calvinistic sense.

YEPES, DIEGO DE. Diego de Yepez, Bishop of Tarragona, whose *Historia particular de la perseucion de Inglaterra* was published in Madrid in 1599.

Appendix

Transcript of a document at Arundel Castle reproduced as Plate IV.

> Theis shalbe to requier you of soche her Ma^{tes} Treasuer as p'n'tly remayneth in your handes, to content and paie unto our loving freinde Sr Arthur Champernon Knighte Viceadmirall of the Countie of Devon' bearer hereof: The some of one hundred M'kes of Lawfull money of England for soche charges as he hathe ben at for sendinge certen shipps to the seas, by our apointme't for her heighnes sp'iall service. And theis our l'res, wth the saide Sr Arthur his bill testefyinge the receipte of the same, shalbe your sufficient Warrannte and Discharge in that behalf. At Hamptoncou'te the xxvj^{th} of January. 1573
>
> To our veary Lovinge Freindes the Treasurer and Chamberleynes of the Exchequier

W. BURGHLEY   E. LYNCOLN   ARUNDELL

F BEDFORD

F KNOLLYS   T. SMITH   FRA: WALSYNGHAM

The signatories are :—

- **W. BURGHLEY**: William Cecil, 1st Baron Burghley (1521-1598), Lord High Treasurer.

- **E. LYNCOLN**: Edward Clinton *alias* Fiennes, 1st Earl of Lincoln (1512-1584/5), Lord High Admiral.

- **ARUNDELL**: Henry FitzAlan, Earl of Arundel (1512-1579/80), whose daughter Mary was the mother of St. PHILIP HOWARD.

- **F. BEDFORD**: Francis Russell, Earl of Bedford (1527-1585), Privy Councillor.

- **F. KNOLLYS**: Sir Francis Knollys (1514?-1596), Treasurer of the Royal Household.

T. SMITH : Sir Thomas Smith (1513-1577), Secretary of State.

FRA : WALSYNGHAM : Sir Francis Walsingham (1530?-1590), Secretary of State.

For Sir Arthur Champernowne, Vice-Admiral of the West, see *Burke's Genealogical and Heraldic History of the Landed Gentry* under Champernowne of Pound.